FREEDOM TO

C000082742

The P(

Divide

WALKING THE MOORS
BETWEEN GREATER MANCHESTER
AND YORKSHIRE

The Pennine Divide

WALKING THE MOORS BETWEEN GREATER MANCHESTER AND YORKSHIRE

Andrew Bibby

The Ramblers

FRANCES LINCOLN

FREEDOM TO ROAM

The Freedom to Roam guides
are dedicated to the memory of
Benny Rothman

Frances Lincoln Ltd, 4 Torriano Mews, Torriano Avenue, London NW5 2RZ
www.franceslincoln.com

The Pennine Divide
Copyright © Andrew Bibby 2005

Photographs on frontispiece, pages 25, 58–9, 78–9, 88–9, 98–9, 101, 112–13 by
Steven Gillis © HD9 Imaging; photographs on pages 18–19, 32–3, 46–7, 106–7, 136–7
© John Morrison; photographs on pages 12–13, 66–7, 82–3, 129 © Andrew Bibby;
photograph on pages 50–51 © Delph Quickstep Contest; photograph on pages 72–3
© Ray Manley; photograph on page 117 © Huddersfield Canal Society;
illustration on page 144 © Martin Bagness

Lyrics from 'The Manchester Rambler' song by Ewan MacColl used by kind permission
of Peggy Seeger and of the publisher Harmony Music Ltd

Maps reproduced from Ordnance Survey mapping on behalf of The Controller
of Her Majesty's Stationery Office © Crown Copyright 100043293 2004

First published by Frances Lincoln 2005

British Library Cataloguing in Publication Data
A catalogue record for this book is available from the British Library

ISBN 0-7112-2500-1
Printed and bound in Singapore by Kyodo Printing Co.
9 8 7 6 5 4 3 2 1

Frontispiece photograph: Eastergate bridge, near Marsden

Contents

Acknowledgments

The author gratefully acknowledges the assistance given him by a wide range of individuals and organizations, and is particularly grateful for the help offered by Kate Conto and Dan French of the Ramblers' Association, and Kate Cave and Fiona Robertson at Frances Lincoln. Also much appreciated has been the assistance offered by Rowena Pemford, Lynn Pegler and Fred Carter (all British Waterways), Mike Rhodes (Peak District National Park), Neil Windett (Kirklees MC), Carl Baron (Tameside MBC), Mary Rodgers (Delph Whit Friday Committee), Richard Humpidge (National Trust), Gwen Goddard, Malcolm Banks, Liz Colquohoun, Brian Lawrence, Terry Norris, Keith Pennyfather, Nigel Smith, Mandy Goth, Phil Hodgson, Richard Leonard, Ian Starkey, Peter Roworth, Bob Gough (Huddersfield Canal Society) and Jane Scullion.

Series introduction

This book, and the companion books in the series, celebrate the arrival in England and Wales of the legal right to walk in open country. The title for the series is borrowed from a phrase much used during the long campaign for this right – Freedom to Roam. For years, it was the dream of many to be able to walk at will across mountain top, moorland and heath, free of the risk of being confronted by a 'Keep Out' sign or being turned back by a gamekeeper.

The sense of frustration that the hills were, in many cases, out of bounds to ordinary people was captured in the song 'The Manchester Rambler' written by one of the best-known figures in Britain's post-war folk revival, Ewan MacColl. The song, which was inspired by the 1932 'mass trespass' on Kinder Scout when walkers from Sheffield and Manchester took to the forbidden Peak District hills, tells the tale of an encounter between a walker, trespassing on open land, and an irate gamekeeper:

He called me a louse, and said 'Think of the grouse',
Well I thought but I still couldn't see
Why old Kinder Scout, and the moors round about
Couldn't take both the poor grouse and me.

The desire, as Ewan MacColl expressed it, was a simple one:

So I'll walk where I will, over mountain and hill
And I'll lie where the bracken is deep,
I belong to the mountains, the clear running fountains
Where the grey rocks rise ragged and steep.

Some who loved the outdoors and campaigned around the time of the Kinder Scout trespass in the 1930s must have thought that the legal right to walk in open country would be won after the Second World War, at the time when the National Parks were being created and the rights-of-way network drawn up. It was not to be. It was another half century before, finally, Parliament passed the Countryside and Rights of Way Act 2000, and the people of England and Wales gained the legal right to take to the hills and the moors. (Scotland has its own traditions and its own legislation.)

We have dedicated this series to the memory of Benny Rothman, one of the leaders of the 1932 Kinder Scout mass trespass who was imprisoned for his part in what was deemed a 'riotous assembly'. Later in his life, Benny Rothman was a familiar figure at rallies called by the Ramblers' Association as once again the issue of access rights came to the fore. But we should pay tribute to all who have campaigned for this goal. Securing greater access to the countryside was one of the principles on which the Ramblers' Association was founded in 1935, and for many ramblers the access legislation represents the achievement of literally a lifetime of campaigning.

So now, at last, we do have freedom to roam. For the first time in several centuries, the open mountains, moors and heaths of England and Wales are legally open for all. We have the protected right to get our boots wet in the peat bogs, to flounder in the tussocks, to blunder and scrabble through the bracken and heather, and to discover countryside which, legally, we had no way of knowing before.

The Freedom to Roam series of books has one aim: to encourage you to explore and grow to love these new areas of the countryside which are now open to us. The right to roam freely – that's surely something to celebrate.

Walking in open country – a guide to using this book

If the right and the freedom to roam openly are so important – perceptive readers may be asking – why produce a set of books to tell you where to go?

So a word of explanation about this series. The aim is certainly not to encourage walkers to follow each other ant-like over the hills, sticking rigidly to a pre-determined itinerary. We are not trying to be prescriptive, instructing you on your walk stile by stile or gate by gate. The books are not intended as instruction manuals but we hope that they will be valuable as *guides* – helping you discover areas of the countryside which you haven't legally walked on before, advising you on routes you might want to take and telling you about places of interest you will pass along the way.

In areas of countryside where it can be tricky to find routes or landmarks, we offer more detailed instructions.

Elsewhere, we are deliberately less precise in our directions, allowing you to choose your own path or line to follow. For each walk, however, there is a recommended core route, and this forms the basis on which the distances given are calculated.

There is, then, an assumption that those who use this book will be comfortable with using a map – and that, in practice, means one of the Ordnance Survey's 1:25 000 Explorer series of maps. As well as referring to the maps in this book, it is worth taking the full OS map with you, to give you a wider picture of the countryside that you will be exploring.

Safety in the hills

Those who are already experienced upland walkers will not be surprised if at this point we put in a note on basic safety in the hills. Walkers need to remember that walking in open country, particularly high country, is different from footpath walking across farmland or more gentle countryside. The main risk for walkers is of being inadequately prepared for changes in the weather. Even in high summer, hail and even snow are not impossible (as you will discover on pages 34–6, Daniel Defoe found this out for himself when he attempted to cross the Pennines in August 1724).

If rain comes, the temperature will drop as well, so it is important to be properly equipped when taking to the hills and to guard against the risk of hypothermia. Fortunately, walkers today have access to a range of wind- and rain-proof clothing which was not available in the eighteenth century. Conversely, in hot weather you should take sufficient water to avoid the risk of dehydration and hyperthermia (dangerous

overheating of the body).

Be prepared for visibility to drop, when (to use the local term) the clag descends on the hills. It is always sensible to take a compass. If you are unfamiliar with basic compass-and-map work, ask in a local outdoor equipment shop whether they have simple guides available or pick the brains of a more experienced walker.

The other main hazard, even for walkers who know the hills well, is that of suffering an accident such as a broken limb. If you plan to walk alone, it is sensible to let someone know in advance where you will be walking and when you expect to be back – the moorland and mountain rescue services which operate in the area covered by this book are very experienced but they are not psychic. Groups of walkers should tackle only what the least experienced or least fit member of the party can comfortably achieve. Take particular care if you intend to take children with you to hill country. And take a mobile phone by all means, but don't assume you can rely on it in an emergency, since some parts of the moors and hills will not pick up a signal. (If you can make a call and are in a real emergency situation, ring 999 – it is the police who coordinate mountain and moorland rescues.)

If this all sounds off-putting, that is certainly not the intention. The guiding principle behind the access legislation is that walkers will exercise their new-won rights with responsibility. Taking appropriate safety precautions is simply one aspect of acting responsibly.

Access land – what you can and can't do

The countryside which is covered by access legislation includes mountain, moor, heath, downland and common land. After the passing of the Countryside and Rights of Way Act 2000, a lengthy mapping process was undertaken, culminating in the production of 'conclusive' maps which identify land which is open for access. These maps (although not intended as guides for walking) can be accessed via the Internet, at www.countrysideaccess.gov.uk. Ordnance Survey maps

Note: Each walk has been graded, on a scale of 👟 to 👟 👟 👟 👟 👟, for the degree of difficulty involved. In general, walks are judged more difficult if they are (a) longer in mileage, and/or (b) involve more rough walking (across open moorland rather than on established footpaths), and/or (c) pose more navigational problems or venture into very unfrequented areas. But bear in mind that all the walks in this book require map-reading competence and some experience of hill walking.

published from 2004 onwards also show access land.

You can walk, run, birdwatch and climb on access land, although there is no new right to camp or to bathe in streams or lakes (or, of course, to drive vehicles). The regulations sensibly insist that dogs, where permitted, are on leads near livestock and during the bird-nesting season (1 March to 31 July). However, grouse moors have the right to ban dogs altogether, and this is what is happening in several other moorland areas elsewhere in the north of England. For more information, watch out for local signs.

Access legislation also does not include the right to ride horses or bikes, though in some areas there may be

pre-existing agreements that allow this. More information is available on the website given above and, at the time of writing, there is also an advice line on 0845 100 3298.

The access legislation allows for some open country to be permanently excluded from the right to roam. 'Excepted' land includes military land, quarries and areas close to buildings, but in addition landowners can apply for other open land to be excluded. Regrettably, two sizeable sections of moorland in the area covered by this book (north of Broadstone Hill near Diggle, and on Deer Hill Moss near Meltham) have been excluded, because of the presence near by of rifle ranges.

To the best of the authors' knowledge, all the walks in

Wimberry Stones and Dovestone reservoir

the Freedom to Roam series are either on legal rights of way or across access land that is included in the official 'conclusive' maps. However, you are asked to bear in mind that the books have been produced right at the beginning of the new access arrangements, before walkers have started to regularly walk the hills and before any teething problems on the ground have been ironed out. For instance, at the time of writing there were still some places where the entry arrangements to access land had not been finalized. As access becomes better established, it may be that minor changes to the routes suggested in these books will become appropriate or necessary. You are asked to remember that we are encouraging you to be flexible in the way you use the guides.

Walkers in open country also need to be aware that landowners have a further right to suspend or restrict access on their land for up to twenty-eight days a year. (In such cases of temporary closure there is normally still access on public holidays and on most weekends.) Notice of closure needs to be given in advance, and the plan is that this information should be readily available to walkers, it is hoped at local information centres and libraries but also on the countryside access website and at the popular entry points to access land This sort of set-up has generally been found to work well in Scotland, where arrangements have been put in place to make sure that walkers in areas where deer hunting takes place can find out when and where hunting is happening.

Walkers will understand the sense in briefly closing small areas of open countryside when, for example, shooting is in progress (grouse shooting begins on 12 August) or when heather burning is taking place in spring. Once again, however, it is too early in the implementation of the access legislation to know how easily walkers in England and Wales will be able to find out about these temporary access closures. It is also too early to know whether landowners will attempt to abuse this power.

In some circumstances, additional restrictions on access can be introduced – for example, on the grounds of nature conservation or heritage conservation, on the advice of English Nature and English Heritage.

Bear these points in mind, but enjoy your walking in the knowledge that any access restrictions should be the exception and not the norm. The Countryside Agency has itself stated that 'restrictions will be kept to a minimum'. If you find access unexpectedly denied while walking in the areas suggested in this book, please accept the restrictions and follow the advice you are given. However, if you feel that access was wrongly denied, please report your experience to the countryside service of the local authority (or National Park authority, in National Park areas), and to the Ramblers' Association.

Finally, there may be occasions when you choose voluntarily not to exercise your freedom to roam. For example, many of the upland moors featured in these books are the homes of ground-nesting birds such as grouse, curlew, lapwing and pipit, who will be building their nests in spring and early summer. During this time, many people will decide to leave the birds in peace and find other places to walk. Rest assured that you will know if you are approaching an important nesting area – birds are good at telling you that they would like you to go away.

Celebrating the open countryside

Despite these necessary caveats, the message from this series is, we hope, clear. Make the most of the new legal rights we have been given – and enjoy your walking.

Introduction

What Pennine divide? Choose a good day, say a bright Sunday morning when the M62 is free from heavy goods traffic, and the Pennine section of the motorway slips by quietly and effortlessly. Or settle back on the train, on the Leeds–Manchester Piccadilly service, and – always assuming, of course, that the trains are running smoothly – it's easy not to pay much attention to the hills being traversed outside. It's almost as though we don't need to take the Pennines into account any more when making our travel plans.

Almost, but not quite. Because there are still times when the Pennine hills draw attention to themselves in no uncertain fashion. There are those winter days when the snow is falling, when traffic is taken off the M62 and when the warning lights at either end of the trans-Pennine A roads, at places like Huddersfield, Marsden, Holmfirth and Saddleworth, are flashing to advise of impassable roads ahead. But in summer, too, when the weather is foul, when the two inside lanes of the M62 are filled with slow-moving lorries and the rain is bouncing off the windscreen, it can be hard work to make the relatively short Pennine crossing.

This is a range of hills, in other words, which can still provide a barrier. Furthermore the divide created by the Pennines is not just a physical one. There are historical and cultural differences which have been created by the presence of the Pennines. There is also a psychological divide – to the extent that people living on one side of the hills much more readily think of travelling to neighbouring towns on their own side than making an equally short trip to a town on the other side.

So *The Pennine Divide* it is, as the title for this book, but since the Pennine backbone stretches a long way through northern England, something needs to be said immediately about the geographical area which this book aims to cover. The focus will be on a relatively short section of the chain – but one where, because there are millions of people living just a short distance away on either side of the hills, the importance of the Pennine divide (and, as we shall see, the importance of being able to cross that divide) becomes particularly significant.

This book's northern boundary conveniently follows the M62 (north of here, the hills and moors above the Calder and Worth valleys and the countryside up to Ilkley and Rombalds Moor are covered in the companion volume in the Freedom to Roam series, *South Pennines and the Bronte Moors*). As for the south, the appropriate place to draw the line is Longdendale, the valley of the Etherow which is now dominated by the Woodhead, Torside and Rhodeswood reservoirs. (Just one walk in the book, Walk 6 to Bleaklow, ventures south below this point, though the walk itself starts in Longdendale.) At Bleaklow and Woodhead the book meets up with two other books in the Freedom to Roam series, those covering the Peak District – the jigsaw, in other words, is completed.

So what is there for walkers to enjoy in our stretch of the Pennines, between the margins of the M62 and Longdendale? Plenty. One quick answer might be: wild moorland, beautiful valleys, peaty bogs and heather-covered slopes, and a fascinating past which has left much for both the archaeologist and the social historian to appreciate.

Arguably this is a section of the Pennines that deserves more attention than it usually receives. One problem is the way in which it straddles the northern boundary of the Peak District National Park and the southern end of the more ill-defined region known as the south Pennines. This means that those guidebooks which focus on the Peak District, and those covering the Calder valley and the southern Pennine moors, both tend to come this way only as something of an afterthought. And yet this is the closest open country for much of eastern Greater Manchester and for important west Yorkshire centres like Huddersfield.

If the 'Pennine divide' of the title provides one theme for this book, there is a second, complementary, theme – and that is the way in which humans have managed, at different times and in different ways, to bridge that divide.

The M62 provides one example: here is Britain's only high-level motorway, the road which when it was built in the 1960s required the civil engineers and construction teams to tackle challenges which they had not had to face anywhere else. Despite the appalling weather conditions they faced (in the much-quoted remark of one engineer, this was when he

Pule Hill, from Buckstones

discovered that rain could actually rain upwards!), there is still, forty years on, a great deal of pride and satisfaction felt by those who had a hand in building the M62. Some say it was the best job they ever had.

But perhaps the M62 is not the right example to start with. If we are to be systematic, we should begin instead with the M712, another important trans-Pennine highway constructed, like the M62, with much hard slog and effort, just a few miles further to the south.

It is understandable if this road name does not immediately ring any bells with today's motorway drivers: M712 is the name given by archaeologists to the Roman road built in the years around AD 79 to link the important military centres of Chester and York. Unlike other important Roman trunk roads in England (Watling Street and Ermine Street are two obvious examples) we don't know what the Romans themselves called this road, which is why archaeological fieldworkers make do with a standard 'M' number notation, devised for Roman roads by the eminent archaeologist and writer I.D. Margary. But despite M712's anonymity in this respect, it was a key part of the Roman transport infrastructure, built at a time when the north of England was inclined to challenge Roman hegemony and was in need of some firm lessons in military might.

Travellers on the high Pennine section of the M712 would have been moving at marching pace, not 70 mph, but the views would have been similar to those from the M62. The Roman road left Manchester running in two relatively straight alignments to Castleshaw, near Saddleworth. From Castleshaw, however, the road took a series of dog-legs over the watershed, crossing what are now the desolate moors of Close Moss and March Haigh Flat before heading off north-eastwards to Cupwith Hill (north of Marsden) on its way, eventually, to York.

We can trace the route of the M712 partly because of the evidence left behind in the ground, in particular the remains of the road's *agger* – that is, the artificial mound, built up using soil and stones, on which the road itself was constructed. In places near Castleshaw the *agger* is clearly visible, as much as three feet (one metre) high and forty to fifty feet (twelve to fifteen metres) across. Castleshaw, in fact, is the place where visitors to the area interested in its Roman past should make their way, for here can be found the excavated remains of one of the garrison forts which the Romans built alongside the Chester–York road. Walk 2 in this book will go that way.

So the Pennine divide was successfully bridged by the Romans almost two thousand years ago. But even this is not necessarily the start of the story. This part of the southern Pennine chain is rich in prehistoric remains, including some going right back to the middle Stone Age, the mesolithic period. W.P.B. Stonehouse, in his book *The Prehistory of Saddleworth*, considers the archaeological evidence in detail and suggests the possibility that even at that period there was significant cross-Pennine communication. As he puts it, 'It is possible that small groups from both east and west of the Pennines watershed visited our hills. Such groups might have belonged to different territories. The narrow watershed between the east and the west in our area might well have been a suitable place for a meeting between these different groups for social purposes (ritual, marriage, barter, etc.).'

This is, inevitably, informed speculation. But as we leave prehistory and the Romans behind and move into medieval and post-medieval times, the information about the way humans criss-crossed the Pennines becomes much more clear-cut. While the M712 route across the Pennines fell into disuse (as happened elsewhere with Roman roads), new routes developed. In particular, for several centuries packhorse trains provided a key element in the creation and development of local transport networks.

Many of the paths developed for the packhorse trade did not in the end turn into roads, which means that they are now available for walkers to enjoy. Walk 1, for example, makes use in part of the Tunshill Lane, an old bridleway which linked Rochdale with the towns on the Yorkshire side of the hills. Walk 12 also follows an old packhorse route, one which was used by many generations of people making their way to and from Marsden – but which nearly disappeared from public use behind 'private' signs early in the twentieth century, as the result of pressure from the landowner (the full story of this early fight for access is told below, on pages 130–31). Eastergate, found at the eastern end of this bridleway, is a particularly attractive former packhorse bridge which is well worth a visit.

It was the coming of turnpike roads from the mid-eighteenth century onwards, however, which established the network of trans-Pennine routes which we still use today. South of the M62, all the major trunk roads that run across the hills are based on turnpike roads. The A672 Denshaw–Ripponden road follows the route of the Oldham–Ripponden turnpike of 1795. The A640 Denshaw–Huddersfield road over Buckstones was originally created for the New Hey–Huddersfield turnpike, established in 1805–6. For the most important crossing of all, at Standedge, where barely half a mile (less than a kilometre) of moorland plateau separates east from west, no less than three turnpike roads were built in the period from 1759 to 1839, each on slightly different alignments. Standedge became a very busy route, much used by regular coach services (horse-drawn, of course) which ran between Manchester and Leeds and other large centres of population (see pages 124–6).

Further south, the lonely A635 Greenfield–Holmfirth road and the busy A628 Longdendale road also follow the routes of turnpike roads. The Longdendale valley, now an important trunk route, was identified early in the turnpike era as a key transport artery and the Manchester–Barnsley turnpike was established through the valley in 1728–31.

Because the turnpikes developed into modern A roads, these are more likely to be used by walkers today to get to the start of their walks, rather than for the walks themselves. But at Standedge the lines of the first and second turnpikes were not maintained and now provide pleasant moorland walking: Walk 11 includes stretches on both these historic routes.

Mention of Standedge inevitably leads to talk of tunnels. After the turnpikes came the canals, and for our area that means the Huddersfield Narrow Canal, the optimistic vision of a trans-Pennine artery which, despite running hopelessly over budget, was nevertheless eventually achieved. Walk 11 follows much of the line of the Standedge canal tunnel, but above ground rather than underground. Nevertheless there is one way in which the Standedge tunnel itself can, in a sense, be 'hiked' – the feature on pages 114–17 explains exactly how.

The Huddersfield canal gave way to the Huddersfield– Manchester railway, which was responsible for three further tunnels through the heart of the Pennines at Standedge. At the south of our area, Longdendale was also utilized for a cross-Pennine rail link, with a series of tunnels built through the hills at Woodhead. The Standedge line remains open, but the Longdendale railway (despite in its time being used as an inter-city route for London–Manchester express services) was unable to survive the railway rationalization process of the 1960s. Like the old packhorse trails, here was a route across the hills which no longer had a need to fulfil.

Unlike the packhorse bridleways, however, the course of the Longdendale railway has found an official new role, as a recreational route for those wanting to enjoy the countryside. (In fact, as will be mentioned later, the Longdendale trail comprises a small part of the very long-distance E8 footpath linking Ireland with Istanbul.) Walk 6, to Bleaklow, briefly makes use of this route at the beginning and end of the circuit.

From Roman times to the present, therefore, there have been a series of trans-Pennine routes which successfully challenged the Pennine divide. By contrast it was only in the 1960s that the first north–south route *along*, rather than across, the hills came about: the now much-loved 'long green trail' of the Pennine Way, dreamed of by Tom Stephenson back in the 1930s and finally achieved partly thanks to the 1949 landmark National Parks and Access to the Countryside Act. Pennine Way walkers enter this part of the Pennines as they descend from Bleaklow's lonely wastes (Walk 6). They cross the Longdendale valley at Crowden (Walks 7 and 8) and head north on their way to notorious Black Hill (Walk 9). Further north they make their way on sections which where appropriate are also utilized for some of the routes in this book: briefly at Redbrook reservoir (Walk 11) and Badger Slacks (Walk 12), at Millstone Edge, Standedge (Walk 2), and finally at Windy Hill and White Hill (Walk 1).

The Pennine Way's younger companion, the Pennine Bridleway (see pages 60–61), has now brought about another north–south artery through these hills, though it opts for a less arduous route on lower ground. As will be discovered, the Pennine Bridleway, like the Pennine Way, turns up like a familiar friend in a number of the walks in this volume.

So now all that is left is to see this countryside for yourself, to enjoy the particular pleasure which comes from being in the open country – even in the wet and the boggy and the desolate places – and, by tackling the walks in this book, to make your own way across the Pennine hills.

Saddleworth Moor

WALK 1

WINDY HILL AND WHITE HILL

DIFFICULTY 🥾🥾 **DISTANCE 9 miles (14.5 km)**

| HOLLINGWORTH LAKE | TUNSHILL LANE | WINDY HILL | WHITE HILL | GREAT HILL | PIETHORNE RESERVOIR | HOLLINGWORTH LAKE |

MAP OS Explorer OL21, South Pennines

STARTING POINT Hollingworth Lake

PARKING In the car park beside the Hollingworth Lake visitors' centre (GR 940151) or in other car parks beside the lake

PUBLIC TRANSPORT Trains to Smithy Bridge or Littleborough (both ¾ mile/1.2 km from start) run from Manchester, Bradford and Leeds. Regular buses to Hollingworth Lake run from Rochdale, Milnrow and Littleborough.

From Hollingworth Lake to the Pennine Way at White Hill. Mainly walking on bridleways and paths, with an (avoidable) short stretch of open moorland.

■ Hollingworth is an artificial rather than a natural lake, but unusually for the south Pennines the motivation behind it was not the need to find drinking water for the Yorkshire and Lancashire mill towns but the requirements of the Rochdale Canal. Naturally enough, without an adequate replacement source of water available the top pounds of the canal would rapidly have become emptied, leaving the barges high and dry.

The Rochdale Canal gained parliamentary approval in 1794 and it was opened in 1804. Hollingworth Lake was the largest of the feeder reservoirs constructed for it, and was made by building three embankments to enclose what had previously been a low-lying area of ground. Since Hollingworth was well below the canal's top pound, the water had to be pumped uphill from the lake through a series of underground and above-ground water courses, to be fed into the canal at Summit Pool. This task was achieved by using a steam-powered engine.

Because there was no need to keep the water pure enough for drinking, Hollingworth Lake was able to develop as an inland resort, the role which it still plays today. In Victorian times Hollingworth became known as the 'weyvers' seaport', attracting large numbers of people from nearby mill towns. An 1860 guide described the 'apparently countless' number of boats on the lake: 'Oars are flashing in the sun, and white sails are fluttering and gliding about . . . The ferry steamer is churning its direct course backwards and forwards betwixt the landing stage and the pleasure gardens on the other side of the water.'

Despite the coldness of the water, swimming was permitted in the nineteenth century and Captain Webb trained here for his pioneering cross-Channel swim of 1875.

▶ Walk along the eastern side of the lake, towards Rakewood. Once past the end of the lake, as the tarmac road becomes a track, turn right towards a rugby clubhouse and into an overgrown lane. After a short distance, turn left off this track to cross the far end of the playing fields, aiming for the prominent hillock of Castle Hill ahead. Once out of the playing fields, turn left to find the footpath along the side of Castle Hill, under the M62 viaduct ❶.

▶ page 30

© Crown Copyright 100043293 2004 ngs

■ Rakewood viaduct is, at its highest, 140 ft (43 m) above the valley bottom. Work began on this stylish engineering feat in 1966, with the twenty concrete pillars which carry the weight of the road erected by the summer of 1967. The total span of the viaduct is approximately 840 ft (250 m).

The viaduct was finished for use by motorway construction traffic early in 1969, and the M62 was officially opened to the public in the autumn of 1971.

▶ Continue along this footpath, gradually climbing. At the top, where a footpath signpost marks a major meeting of paths, turn left, following the route of the Pennine Bridleway. This is the old packhorse route known as Tunshill Lane.

After about ½ mile (0.8 km), as you approach Turf Hill ❷, turn back sharp left to pick up another old track, signposted to Windy Hill. Continue for about 1½ miles (2.5 km), until you reach the communications mast at Windy Hill ❸.

■ The M62 is still very close by, but in a cutting about 120 ft (36 m) deep.

▶ Turn on to the Windy Hill access road, and almost immediately right to pick up the Pennine Way. Cross the A672 Ripponden–Denshaw road, and continue on the Pennine Way as far as the Ordnance Survey trig point at White Hill ❹.

The suggested route here is to leave the Pennine Way and head south-westwards across the open moor towards Great Hill. This is rough ground, though with luck a series of animal trods (faint paths) can be found running in the right direction ❺. Beyond Great Hill, follow the fence line down, continuing in the same south-westerly direction. (In poor weather, or if you would prefer to stay on recognized paths, continue on the Pennine Way after White Hill until the A640 and return by the bridleway beside Readycon Dean reservoir.)

Cross the A672 near the Ram's Head pub and restaurant, and continue down the hill to Piethorne reservoir ❻.

■ Piethorne is the largest of the five reservoirs in the Ogden valley, built to hold water for the people of Oldham. Piethorne was the first to be constructed, and was completed in 1866. It holds up to 44 million gallons of water (as well as a good supply of trout).

Water arrives in Piethorne from various sources, including from the Blackstone Edge reservoir several miles north of the M62. Blackstone Edge is higher up, so the water is brought down by gravity feed.

The small building passed to the right at the head of Piethorne reservoir was formerly a limehouse. Lime was stored here, to be added to the main feeder stream to the reservoir, to reduce the acidity of the water.

▶ Immediately past Piethorne reservoir, turn left into Old House Ground plantation (locally known as Bluebell Wood). Follow the footpath through the woods and beyond, until the ruins of Binns farmhouse are reached, above Kitcliffe reservoir **7**.

■ Binns was a significant settlement in medieval times. It was compulsorily purchased in 1867 by Oldham Corporation, to ensure that the purity of drinking water in the reservoirs below was not contaminated.

▶ Beyond Binns turn half-right up an old bridleway, and then shortly turn left to take the path up Town Hill to the pylon at the top. Beyond, drop down to cross Tunshill Lane and retrace your steps taking the outward path back to Hollingworth Lake.

The M62 motorway through the Pennines

Snow in summer

It can be cold in the Pennines even in summer. Fortunately, though, most walkers in the hills these days don't have to contend with the atrocious weather conditions which faced Daniel Defoe in August in 1724.

Defoe had arrived in Rochdale from Liverpool and Bury, and was planning to cross to Halifax on the Yorkshire side of the Pennines. Although it was the middle of August the hills were, according to Defoe, covered with snow and the cold was 'very acute and piercing'. Luckily, relief was at hand:

> We found, as in all those northern countries is the case, that people had an extraordinary way of mixing the warm and the cold very happily together; for the store of good ale which flows plentifully in the most mountainous part of this country seems abundantly to make up for all the inclemencies of the season or difficulties of travelling.

Thus fortified, and after an overnight stop, 'We mounted the hills, and though the snow which had fallen in the night lay a little upon the ground, yet we thought it was not much; and the morning being calm and clear, we had no apprehension of an uneasy passage.'

Defoe and two travelling companions, together with two servants, turned down an offer of help in finding the route made to them in Rochdale. But: 'When we began to mount the hills . . . we found the wind began to rise, and the higher we went the more wind.' Very quickly it became apparent that the decision to reject assistance had been foolish: 'As we ascended higher it began to snow again, that is to say, we ascended into that part where it was snowing, and had, no doubt, been snowing all night, as we could easily see by the thickness of the snow.'

Near the top, Defoe's party encountered white-out conditions:

It is not easy to express the consternation we were in when we came up near the top of the mountain; the wind blew exceeding hard, and blew the snow so directly in our faces, and that so thick, that it was impossible to keep our eyes open to see our way. The ground also was so covered with snow, that we could see no track, or when we were in the way, or when out; except when we were shewed it by a frightful precipice on one hand, and uneven ground on the other.

There was worse to come: 'In the middle of this difficulty, and as we began to call to one another to turn back again, not knowing what dangers might still be before us, came a surprizing clap of thunder, the first that ever I heard in a storm of snow, or, I believe, ever shall; nor did we perceive any lightning to precede the thunder, as must naturally be the case; but we supposed the thick falling of the snow might prevent our sight.' At this point, the party stopped and pondered whether to retreat to Rochdale. However, one of the servants had gone on a little way ahead, and reported back that he could see the way down into the Yorkshire side of the hills. They pressed on:

There was indeed the mark or face of a road on the side of the hill, a little turning to the left north; but it was so narrow, and so deep a hollow place on the right, whence the water descending from the hills made a channel at the bottom, and looked as the beginning of the river, that the depth of the precipice, and the narrowness of the way, look'd horrible to us; after going a little way in it, the way being deeper and deeper, so we resolved to alight and lead our horses, which we did for about a mile, though the violence of the wind and snow continuing, it was both very troublesome and dangerous.

The rivers had swollen with water, and at one point they had to wade knee-deep through a stream. Fortunately, however, the more they descended, the better the weather. Eventually they were in sight of farmhouses and considered the worst of the journey behind them. Nevertheless:

> We soon found our selves mistaken in the matter; for we had not gone fifty yards beyond the brook and houses adjacent, but we found the way began to ascend again, and soon after to go up very steep, till in about half a mile we found we had another mountain to ascend, in our apprehension as bad as the first, and before we came to the top of it, we found it began to snow, too, as it had done before.

Defoe's battles with the unseasonal weather eventually ended with the party safely down the valley, in Halifax, where no doubt he made more use of the 'good ale' he had enjoyed in Rochdale.

The route Defoe took that day must have been close to that of the present-day M62, but the exact path he followed has been the subject of debate. He mentions that he passed over Blackstone Edge and reached Halifax by way of Sowerby and Sowerby Bridge, which suggests that he took the long-established route through Littleborough and over what is now known as the Roman road. But author and historian Keith Parry, in his book *Trans-Pennine Heritage*, has another theory: he believes that Defoe may have used the packhorse route known as Tunshill Lane up to Windy Hill and Blackstone Edge. Be warned that this is the same route as that taken in Walk 1 in this book – though it is hoped that anyone tackling this walk today will have the sun to escort them rather than the snow.

WALK 2

CASTLESHAW

DIFFICULTY 🥾 🥾 **DISTANCE** 4½ miles (7.2 km)

CASTLESHAW   WOOD FARM   MOOR LANE   PENNINE WAY (MILLSTONE EDGE)   ROMAN FORT   CASTLESHAW

MAPS OS Explorer OL21, South Pennines; OS Explorer OL1, The Peak District – Dark Peak area

STARTING POINT Castleshaw Centre car park, off the A62 north of Delph (GR 996091)

PARKING In the car park beside the Castleshaw Centre

PUBLIC TRANSPORT Buses between Huddersfield/Marsden and Oldham/Saddleworth pass within ½ mile (0.8 km). Alight near the A670/A62 junction north of Diggle.

A pleasant horseshoe route high above the Castleshaw reservoirs, taking in a short stretch of the Pennine Way at Millstone Edge, Standedge. One stretch of (avoidable) rougher walking.

▶ Leave the Castleshaw car park, crossing the lower reservoir dam and following the lane to Wood Farm ❶. Here turn left, and continue across another track into a field, following the left side of a stream. At the top, turn left into Low Gate Lane, and immediately right on to Moor Lane.

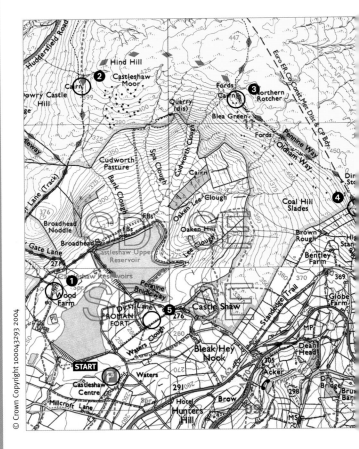

© Crown Copyright 100043293 2004

■ For a short distance, the route now follows the Pennine Bridleway (see pages 60–61). This section of the Derbyshire–Northumberland trail was formally opened by the Countryside Agency in 2004. The mounting block commemorates Edith Boon, who campaigned locally for horse riders.

▶ Continue up Moor Lane and on to the moor, as the Pennine Bridleway turns off to the left.

■ In proposals announced in 2003, the area of moorland to the left was lined up by United Utilities as a suitable site for the construction of a nine-turbine wind farm. Five turbines were scheduled for land directly to the east of Moor Lane, with a further four slightly further north. However, United Utilities' proposals immediately attracted local opposition, with one councillor calling the Castleshaw valley 'Saddleworth's jewel in the crown'. At the time of writing, the result of the proposal is not known. However, the next few years are likely to see many more plans for wind farms in upland areas of Britain, particularly (as here) in areas of the south Pennines which are outside the limits of the National Park.

▶ Shortly after a cairn ❷, the moorland path swings east around the head of the valley,

and meets up with the Pennine Way ❸. Continue past the outcrops of gritstone rock to the trig point at Millstone Edge ❹.

■ Just before the trig point is reached, on a prominent rock facing down to the valley is a memorial to Ammon Wrigley. (Look out for the arrow pointer with the letters 'AW'.) Ammon Wrigley was born in 1861 and died in 1946. He was both a gifted local historian and antiquarian and a poet and writer, whose best-known work is probably his *Songs of a Moorland Parish*. His works were set to music by the modern British composer Arthur Butterworth in his *Moorland Symphony*.

Wrigley also loved roaming the Pennine hills, walking over what he called 'the green miles and the grey' above Saddleworth:

There's no better earth for roaming
And no better folks I say.

There is a statue of Ammon Wrigley in Uppermill.

▶ Leave the Pennine Way at the trig point, and head straight down the hill, keeping to the right of the moorside wall. (To avoid the next stretch of open moorland walking, use one of the field footpaths and lanes slightly further to the east.) Continue right to the end of the moor, turning right on to the road at the bottom. At the houses at Castleshaw, take the footpath almost straight ahead (rather than turning half-right into Dirty Lane) and walk up to the site of the Castleshaw Roman fort (GR 999096) ❺.

■ The Roman fort at Castleshaw was built alongside the Roman road which ran from Chester and Manchester to York. From the fort the road climbed to Standedge, close to where the Millstone Edge trig point now is, then turned sharp north-west along the watershed before turning north-east again, to pass March Haigh Flat near what is now March Haigh reservoir.

The fort itself was first constructed about AD 79. More precisely, there were two forts, a larger fort which was only occupied for a relatively short time (until perhaps AD 90), and a smaller 'fortlet', constructed within the ramparts of the earlier fort close to the start of the second century AD and designed to hold a smaller size of garrison.

The Roman site at Castleshaw was first reported in a paper presented to the Royal Society in 1751, and the site has been excavated on several occasions (including, in 1897, by Ammon Wrigley). Interestingly, excavations on the same site in 1964 also found evidence of Bronze Age settlement, long before the Romans came. Remains of about five beaker vessels were found.

▶ From the Roman fort, walk down the hill to return to the starting point.

Yorkshire for ever

When they were drawing up the maps for the local government administrative changes in 1974, there can't have been much discussion about where to draw the boundary between West Yorkshire and Greater Manchester – they just put it straight along the Pennine watershed.

Logical, straightforward, simple. But, unfortunately, also controversial. The mill villages which together make up the community of Saddleworth may be on the western slopes of the Pennines, but they were also historically part of Yorkshire, and history – particularly in Yorkshire – matters a great deal.

The old West Riding of Yorkshire was an unwieldy beast, a vast administrative area based on Wakefield which stretched from Sheffield and Doncaster in the south to Ripon in the north. In the west, the boundary in several places extended far beyond the Pennines, so that the West Riding included great swathes of territory in the Forest of Bowland which were transferred in 1974 to Lancashire, as well as a smaller area near Sedbergh which went to Cumbria.

As part of this general rearrangement of the old historic boundaries, Saddleworth too was told to leave Yorkshire, in this case to join up with Oldham in a new entity to be called Greater Manchester. Residents of Diggle, Delph, Dobcross, Uppermill and the other mill villages which together make up the community of Saddleworth would have to get used to having a new address – and some of them were distinctly unhappy at the prospect. Didn't anyone realize that they were Yorkshire men and women, born and bred?

More than thirty years later, some are still unhappy. The campaign to assert that, whatever the government may say, Saddleworth remains as always in 'Real Yorkshire' is led by the Saddleworth White Rose Society, which loses no opportunity to argue its case. Yorkshire, it maintains, is an historic entity, not simply an area demarcated by local government administrative boundaries.

The White Rose Society appears to have some allies locally. Saddleworth's parish council, for example, voted in 2003 for the council's official postal address to be given as 'Civic Hall, Lee Street, Uppermill, Saddleworth, Yorkshire'. And in recent years, Saddleworth has enthusiastically joined in the tradition, which began to develop in all three of Yorkshire's old ridings after the 1974 changes, of celebrating Yorkshire Day on 1 August.

This is the day to get out the white rose flags and pennants and bang the drum for Yorkshire. As the Saddleworth White Rose Society put it in the run-up to the 2004 event, 'with Yorkshire flags flying and brass bands playing, this will make a strong and clear statement to spectators watching and the local press that the people of Saddleworth are proud to be Yorkshire folk'.

Say it loud enough and those people 'across the county boundary' in Oldham might just get the message – even if the council tax bills continue to be posted in Oldham Town Hall.

WALK 3

POTS AND PANS

DIFFICULTY 👢 👢   **DISTANCE** 4½ miles (7.2 km)

POBGREEN (SADDLEWORTH)   BROADSTONE HILL   SLADES ROCKS   UPPER WOOD EDGE   ALDERMAN'S HILL   POTS AND PANS STONE/ WAR MEMORIAL   POBGREEN

MAP OS Explorer OL1, The Peak District – Dark Peak area

STARTING POINT Pobgreen church, east of Uppermill, Saddleworth (GR 008064)

PARKING Possible near Pobgreen church

PUBLIC TRANSPORT Uppermill (about 1 mile/1.6 km away) is served by regular buses from Oldham, Manchester, Huddersfield and Ashton. Bus 354 (Rochdale–Ashton, three services a day, no Sunday service) runs to within ½ mile (0.8 km) of Pobgreen.

A relatively gentle circuit of the hillside above Uppermill taking in a series of viewpoints, each with subtly different views to enjoy. (Choose a day with good visibility!)

■ The walk begins beside Saddleworth's parish church, built in 1831 and dedicated to St Chad. The saint was born in Northumbria, probably in the 620s, but he is associated more with the Midlands kingdom of Mercia than with the north; he became the first Bishop of Lichfield in 669 and died three years later.

Note, in front of the church, the set of village stocks which carry the date 1698.

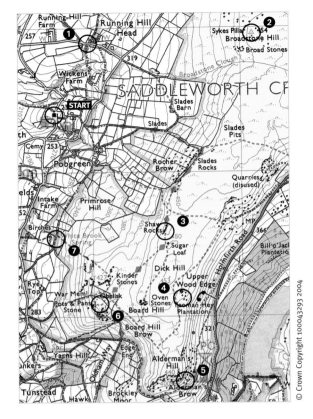

© Crown Copyright 100043293 2004

Saddleworth's church is one of the venues visited by the Saddleworth rushcart during the annual rushcart weekend festivities, held in August. This tradition, revived in 1975, involves parading a cart piled high with rushes (and with an unfortunate volunteer perched on the very top) around the villages of Saddleworth. Beer and morris dancing both seem to play an important part in the success of the event.

▶ Take the overgrown lane east from the corner of the church (not the footpath next to it which runs diagonally up the hillside). Follow the lane ahead, past farm buildings and the front of Ivy Bank Farm, and then turn left, picking up the field footpath running in a northerly direction.

■ Briefly the route follows the Oldham Way, a 40-mile (64-km) circular walk promoted by Oldham Council. This being Saddleworth, home of Yorkshire irredentists (see pages 41–2), you may notice that certain of the 'Oldham Way' signs on this stretch of path have the word Oldham scratched out.

This part of the Oldham Way is included in one of the two alternative routes which make up the British part of the E2 European long-distance walking route from Galway to Nice.

▶ Continue on the footpath until a tarmac road is reached ❶. Turn right, and walk up the hill. At the top, continue ahead into an old lane. Carry on up this lane into open country, leaving the wall in due course to follow the left side of Broadstone Clough uphill.

Near the top of the hill, make for the trig point at Broadstone Hill ❷.

■ Broadstone Hill at 1489 ft (454 m) is the first of several viewpoints on this walk. To the north-east the distinctive shape of Pule Hill (Walk 11) can be seen, with the cliff face of Shooter's Nab on Deer Hill Moss (Walk 10) also visible further to the right. To the north-west, the Standedge ridge followed by the Pennine Way north from Millstone Edge stands out clearly, while to the left one of the two Castleshaw reservoirs is just in sight (Walk 2). Over to the west are the tower blocks of Oldham and, further away, Manchester.

▶ From Broadstone Hill, turn back to follow the well-walked path which runs southwards along the ridge of the hill, passing the gritstone outcrop called Slades Rocks. The Shaw Rocks just beyond ❸, perched at the edge of the hillside, offer another place to stop to admire the view. From here, it is readily apparent how the hills enfold Uppermill and the other Saddleworth settlements.

▶ page 48

Winter in Saddleworth

A detailed guidebook is not really required to enjoy the hillside south of the Shaw Rocks, with plenty of opportunity to wander at will. But the suggested route is to cross the hillside, passing the rounded boulder known as the Sugar Loaf, to make for the prominent rocky outcrop at Upper Wood Edge, on the eastern side ❹.

■ From here, the view switches from north and west to east. Ahead and below are the three reservoirs of the Greenfield valley: Dovestone to the right, Yeoman Hey ahead and Greenfield itself to the left. Directly ahead, above Yeoman Hey, is the hillside of Ashway Hey (Walk 4 offers a chance to explore this fine hill ridge).

▶ Take the path which runs along the brow towards Alderman's Hill, at the southernmost point of the hill ❺. Here the view has changed yet again, to include Alphin Pike just across the valley and the long clough of Chew Brook making its way up the hillside from Dovestone reservoir.

Turn back, to make for the obelisk to the north-west. This prominent landmark is Saddleworth's memorial to the dead of the two world wars ❻.

■ A few yards (metres) from the obelisk is the outcrop known as the Pots and Pans stone. Some imaginative people will tell you that the rocks really do resemble kitchen utensils. Perhaps . . .
It is worth clambering up the rock to see the natural water-filled cavities found at the top.

▶ From the obelisk, head away from the Pots and Pans stone along a set of old iron railings, aiming to pick up a path leading north-westwards down the hillside, towards Birches farmhouse ❼. Just before Birches, take the footpath running northwards close to the foot of the open hillside. (Alternatively, keep on the hillside a little longer, scrambling down the side of Primrose Hill to pick up the same path at the foot.) Follow the path back to the cottages at Pobgreen.

Whit Friday in Saddleworth

There can't be many people in the country now who know when it's Whit Friday.

But the community of Saddleworth is an exception. Here Whit Friday – it moves around the calendar and can fall any time from mid-May to mid-June – is one of the highlights of the year, and some would claim it as the most important day of all. Schools close and local people, adults and children alike, spill out on to the streets. Whit Friday in Saddleworth means one thing: the traditional Whit Friday brass band competition.

This isn't just a local event. In recent years, upwards of a hundred bands have taken part in the day's events, some travelling the length of England to participate. (Some come from overseas, too.) There is serious prestige – and some serious prize money – attached to winning the overall championship, but it's also an occasion for socializing, for meeting up with players from other bands and for having a drink or two to celebrate your successful performances – or maybe to drown your disappointment.

Saddleworth unusually is not a single town but rather a collection of villages strung out along the Pennine edge, and each village traditionally puts on its own competition. This means that you have to organize your timetable efficiently and persuade your bus driver to tackle the narrow, hilly lanes so that your band can dash from one competition to another: Uppermill as soon as possible after the start at 4.30pm, let's say, then down to Greenfield thereafter, across to Grotton and Lydgate perhaps, with Dobcross, Delph and Denshaw for the evening.

Although the number of individual village competitions can vary from year to year, these days there are typically about ten to

▶ page 52

The centre of Delph, Whit Friday festival

twelve to choose from. Some bands try to cram in as many as they can (people still recall how the Fairey Band in 1988 managed to play at thirteen events – and what's more they came in the top three placings in all thirteen). But, assuming you want to qualify for the overall area competition, you have to perform in at least six of the venues.

The band competitions normally get under way at 4.30pm, and then carry on right through the evening. Each village competition accepts band registrations up to about 10.30 or 11pm, and this can mean in some places that the final band is still performing after midnight. Things have got slightly easier these days thanks to mobile phones: bands ring up a few minutes in advance to check how long the waiting time is at their preferred next venue. But there is still plenty of piling into and out of buses to be done – as well, of course, as plenty of marching and playing.

As you would expect, the rules are taken seriously. Each band gets to play two pieces of music in each village, one as they march to take up their position and a second (and this is the one which really matters) when they are in place on the rostrum – or whatever patch of ground passes for a stage. Close at hand but out of sight, perhaps in the darkened upstairs room of a pub or church hall, or in a caravan, is the adjudicator. The task of the adjudicators is to assess and rank all the bands they hear, without of course knowing which are the top-notch favourites and which are the scratch outfits. All they have to help are their ears and a copy of the score of the march being performed, which is rushed to the hiding place by a helper. It's not easy. As David Read, an experienced Whit Friday adjudicator told performers at Delph in 2004, 'Take my word for it, I have done both and playing is easier and more enjoyable!'

But as well as the band competition, there's another, less overt, competition going on at the same time, and that is between the villages themselves. Naturally enough, each works hard to try to ensure that their event goes off perfectly. For the volunteer committees which organize the competitions, Whit Friday is the culmination of what is often a whole year of planning and preparation.

Why Whit Friday, an apparently random date in the calendar which is just an ordinary working day for the rest of Britain? The reason, predictably, is tradition. The week after Whit Sunday was historically a holiday week in the mill towns of the north-west, when the mills and other workplaces would close. Even though the Whitsun holiday tradition has died away (even the residual Whit Monday bank holiday was abolished in 1967, when it was replaced by the spring bank holiday), Saddleworth keeps to the old ways. After all, there have been brass band competitions in this part of the Pennine edge since at least 1884.

Saddleworth's Whit Friday has been called the greatest free show on earth. But first-time visitors need to check their diaries carefully to avoid the embarrassment of turning up on the wrong day: just remember that Whit Friday falls exactly eight weeks after Good Friday.

WALK 4

DOVESTONE

DIFFICULTY 🥾 🥾 🥾   **DISTANCE** 10½ miles (17 km)

DOVESTONE RESERVOIR — ALPHIN PIKE — WIMBERRY ROCKS — CHEW RESERVOIR — DISH STONE BROW — FOX STONE — ASHWAY ROCKS — GREEN-FIELD RESERVOIR — DOVESTONE RESERVOIR

MAP OS Explorer OL1, The Peak District – Dark Peak area

STARTING POINT Dovestone reservoir, near Greenfield

PARKING In the Dovestone reservoir car park (GR 013036)

PUBLIC TRANSPORT Trains to Greenfield station (1½ miles/ 2.5 km from start) from Manchester, Leeds, Wakefield and Huddersfield. Buses to Greenfield village (¾ mile/1.2 km from start) run from Oldham and Ashton; there are occasional buses (no Sunday service) from Rochdale.

A classic Dark Peak horseshoe ridge walk, high above the Dovestone, Yeoman Hey and Greenfield reservoirs.

■ Dovestone reservoir is now an established part of the landscape, but was only completed in 1967. Yeoman Hey, above it, is the earliest

of the three reservoirs in the Greenfield valley, having been constructed in the 1880s.

▶ From the car park, walk along Bradbury Lane. Just before Fern Lee Farm, turn sharp back left on to Intake Lane. Halfway to the woods ❶, turn right on to the open moors, scrambling up the hillside beside a stone wall. The target is the trig point and cairn at Alphin Pike, about 650 ft (200 m) above. Be warned that there is a false summit before the trig point is reached ❷.

■ Alphin Pike at 1538 ft (469 m) is one of the first significant hills east of the Manchester conurbation, and as a consequence it offers excellent views down towards the city. The trig point itself is almost lost in a larger cairn.

▶ From the trig point, a relatively well-walked path continues along the brow. When this splits, keep to the left, enjoying the views down to Dovestone reservoir . The path leads to the impressive Wimberry Rocks outcrop ❸.

■ A tragic air crash occurred here on 19 August 1949, when a BEA flight from Belfast to Manchester ploughed into the hillside just below the brow of the hill. The plane was a Dakota, formerly used by the RAF and converted to civilian use. It was carrying twenty-nine passengers, with a crew of three.

According to Ron Collier and Roni Wilkinson, the authors of the two-volume *Dark Peak Aircraft Wrecks*, the most likely explanation for the accident was human error, with the pilot convinced that he was on a flight trajectory slightly to the west of the one his plane was in fact following. He had been cleared for landing at Manchester just before the crash, which took place at about 1pm. Farmers and mill workers from Greenfield rushed to the hillside, and eight passengers were saved.

Ron Collier has made a detailed study of aircraft accidents in the Dark Peak area, and his research has been brought together in the two much-revised books. The books have started a (somewhat macabre) trend for walking to the crash sites.

▶ Continue on the path along the brow as it runs up the side of the Chew Brook valley, eventually arriving at Chew reservoir ❹.

© Crown Copyright 100043293 2004

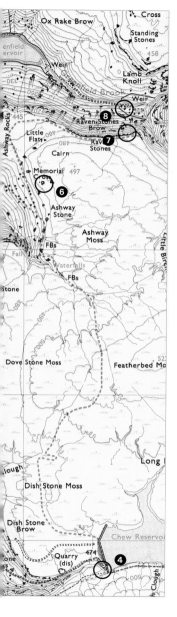

■ Chew reservoir, hidden high up the Chew valley, was constructed in 1912.

▶ Walk across the reservoir dam, ignoring the tarmac of Chew Road which comes up from the valley bottom. Turn left just before the end of the dam to find the defined path which runs off along the ridge on the north side of Chew valley. Continue on this path around Dish Stone Brow, enjoying the views back to Wimberry Rocks and Alphin Pike and down to Dovestone reservoir.

The path continues, in places crossing bare peat, towards the outcrops of rocks at the brow of the hill.

■ The large solitary Fox Stone ❺ at the edge of the brow has had a cairn built over it. On the side of the stone is an unostentatious plaque commemorating two climbers, Brian Toase and Tom Morton, who were killed in the Dolomites in 1972.

▶ Carry on along the side of the hill, following the path which bends round to the east up the side of Dove Stone Clough. Follow the path over the stream, continuing on to the moors on the north side of the clough. (For a shorter walk, it's possible to drop down at this point to Dovestone reservoir below.)

Carry on along the path which heads towards Ashway Rocks. To visit the Celtic-style memorial cross on the hillside above ❻, leave the path shortly before reaching the rocks, scrambling up the hill.

■ Grouse shooting can be dangerous for your health! This sombre cross was erected to record the death in a nineteenth-century shooting accident of James Platt, MP for Oldham. The Platt country mansion was Ashway Gap House, just at the foot of the hill below, beside what would later become Dovestone reservoir. It was an extraordinary Gothic confection, complete with crenellated fortifications and a tower. The house, which at one stage was used to house Italian prisoners of war, was demolished in 1981.

▶ Follow the ridge path beyond Ashway Rocks, turning east past another rocky outcrop known as the Raven Stones ❼. The route now runs high up above the Greenfield valley.

At almost the last of the Raven Stones, look for a climbers' path which drops down the hillside towards the water company's track below. Turn left on to the track ❽, and follow it down to the Greenfield and Yeoman Hey reservoirs. Continue through the pleasant woodland beside the Dovestone reservoir to make your way back to the starting point.

Looking down to the Dovestone reservoir

The Pennine Bridleway

The Pennine Way, formally opened in 1965, was Britain's first official long-distance trail. Now, forty years on, it has been joined by the Pennine Bridleway, the latest such route. This new trail, which has been opening in stages in recent years, runs all the way up from Middleton Top in Derbyshire through the south Pennines, the Yorkshire Dales and eastern Cumbria to Byrness in Northumberland.

It's a route that's been particularly designed for horse riders and cyclists – not a single stile or kissing gate to be negotiated, for example – and it tends to keep to slightly lower ground than the original Pennine Way, which heads over almost every peaty summit it can find. The Bridleway route weaves in and out of the western foothills of the south Pennines, and its distinctive marker posts will be spotted at, for example, Hollingworth Lake (Walk 1), Castleshaw (Walk 2) and Walkerwood (Walk 5).

The Pennine Bridleway is very much the result of one person's vision. Mary Towneley, a keen horsewoman who lived in Cliviger near Burnley, knew that paths over the Pennine hills had once been arteries for packhorse trains. She also knew that many of the old packhorse routes and bridleways had disappeared or had been registered as footpaths, rendering them inaccessible to riders. Why not, she thought, bring some of these old routes back to life and provide for the first time in Britain an opportunity for riders to have a real long-distance off-road experience?

With help from the British Horse Society, she researched the old routes and campaigned for them to be made available again to riders, but after many years of effort had little to show for her pains. Then, in 1985, she hit on a new tactic. With two friends, she would set out to prove that it was still possible to ride the length of the Pennines.

Mary Towneley's ride started in Corbridge in Northumberland and ended 250 miles (400 km) or so to the south in Ashbourne in Derbyshire. Planning the route, which in some places used tracks which had not been ridden for more than a hundred years, took eighteen months and at times her journey was anything but easy. But there were compensations, too. Speaking a few years later, she described one moment of great pleasure when, after days negotiating the Pennine moors, she had reached the Eden valley in Cumbria: 'All of a sudden you look down and there is a beautiful lush valley ahead. It's like dropping into heaven,' she said.

Having completed her ride, Mary Towneley wanted others to have a similar taste of the paradise she had found. She lobbied the Countryside Commission, as it then was, and found that the door was opening to her idea. In 1988 the commission funded an initial feasibility study into the Pennine Bridleway, with two members of staff trying to establish exactly where the route should go. Their proposals were first published in 1990, and thereafter followed a lengthy period of discussion and negotiation. In many places, both legal and construction work was necessary to create new bridleways – and not every landowner was sympathetic to the idea. For a period the whole idea of a trans-Pennine bridleway route seemed at risk.

But eventually the work came to fruition. By 2004, the southern section from Derbyshire to West Yorkshire was available for the public to use, and 2008 is the target date for the whole route to Northumberland to be open. Sadly, Mary Towneley died before she had a chance to make a celebratory ride, but it is entirely fitting that the very first section of bridleway to have been opened, the 47-mile (75-km) loop in the south Pennine countryside, carries her name.

WALK 5

WALKERWOOD AND WILD BANK

DIFFICULTY 👟 👟   DISTANCE 5 miles (8 km)

| WALKERWOOD RESERVOIR | HARRIDGE PIKE | HIGHER SWINESHAW RESERVOIR | HOLLINGWORTHALL MOOR | WILD BANK | WALKERWOOD RESERVOIR |

MAP OS Explorer OL1, The Peak District – Dark Peak area

STARTING POINT Walkerwood reservoir/Country Park, Brushes Road, Stalybridge (GR 986990)

PARKING Beside the reservoir dam

PUBLIC TRANSPORT Buses pass the Huddersfield Road/Brushes Road junction (about ½ mile/0.8 km from the Walkerwood reservoir) from Stalybridge and Mossley and also from Manchester, Oldham and Ashton. Stalybridge station, a further mile (1.6 km) away, is served by trains from Leeds, Manchester, Wakefield and Huddersfield.

Two great viewpoints (one of which has been accessible to the public only since 2004) at the start and the finish of this walk, and in between a pleasant circumnavigation of the four reservoirs in the Brushes valley. This far-western corner of the Pennines deserves to be better known.

▶ The first target for this walk is Harridge Pike, to the north of Walkerwood reservoir. Harridge has become open to walkers only since the introduction of access legislation, and at the time of writing there are no obvious routes to the top. This may change as more people walk this way.

For the time being, therefore, the suggested route follows the track along the northern shoreline of the reservoir for a short way. Double back up the footpath coming in from the north-west, and then turn north-east ❶, to take the woodland track above Brushes Farm. The track continues through a gate. At this point either turn directly on to the moor, initially following the wall boundary, or (probably the preferable route) continue along the track. This passes for a short while under a power line, before continuing along the hillside above Brushes reservoir (this part of the track is not currently shown on OS maps). Remain with the track as it finally bends round to the north, and then try to find a sheep path heading towards Harridge Pike. The last few yards (metres) may involve some rough walking ❷.

■ Harridge Pike (1295 ft/ 395 m) is a fine viewpoint offering views across the eastern Manchester conurbation and beyond.

There is considerable evidence that the Harridge Pike hillside was occupied in prehistoric times. Just to the south of the Pike is a site where large numbers of flints and flint blades have been discovered, suggesting that there was a tool workshop here in mesolithic (middle Stone Age) times. There is also a strong probability of later activity: roughly 200 yards (200 m) due east of Harridge Pike — on the higher ground which this route crosses after leaving the Pike — is the site of a likely Bronze Age funerary barrow and cairn.

▶ From Harridge Pike cross roughly eastwards, aiming for the slightly higher ground marked on OS maps with a spot height at 381 m.

Just beyond, you will meet a very defined footpath. Turn right, and follow the path down to Higher Swineshaw reservoir ❸.

■ Higher Swineshaw reservoir is the highest and wildest of

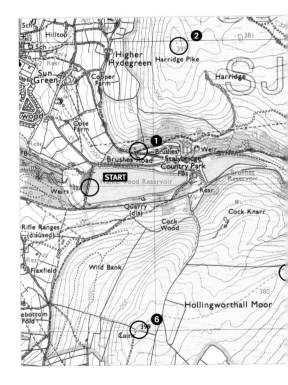

the four reservoirs in the Brushes valley. It was built in 1869.

▶ Take the track over the reservoir dam, briefly following the route of the Pennine Bridleway. Immediately past the dam, turn right, following a well-used track high up above

Lower Swineshaw reservoir **4**. When the right of way turns left, continue straight ahead on a concessionary track. The path briefly crosses a field and then continues across open country, aiming for the heart of Hollingworthall Moor **5**.

Cross Hollingworthall Moor, to arrive at the trig point at Wild

© Crown Copyright 100043293 2004

Bank. At 1309 ft (399 m), Wild Bank is just a little higher than Harridge Pike ❻.

■ As you cross Hollingworthall Moor, suddenly the views open up to the south and – weather permitting, of course – they are magnificent. There,

below, is Tintwistle and the start of the Longdendale valley. Beyond is Glossop, and above Glossop the powerful outline of Bleaklow. Further on can be seen Kinder Edge and the whole western edge of the Kinder plateau. Further still are the moors beyond Hayfield.

The views to be seen from Hollingworthall Moor and Wild Bank have been enjoyed for generations. Here, for example, is a trade directory for Stalybridge (or rather 'Stayley Bridge') from 1825:

> The views from the summit of 'The Wild Bank', elevated as it is thirteen hundred feet above sea level, are very extensive, and, though the axe of the woodman has prostrated the stately oaks, which in the time of the Staveleighs, and for several ages afterwards clothed the neighbouring valleys, yet there is still much here of grandeur and beauty.

Like Harridge, Wild Bank is rich in prehistoric sites, including two funerary cairns dating from the Bronze Age, which may be found close to the trig point (one of these is marked on OS maps, while the other is a very short distance to the east of the trig point).

▶ From the summit of Wild Bank, the easiest route down the hillside is to continue on the path straight ahead, dropping down off the moor in the direction of Flaxfield Farm. At the bottom, turn right and follow a track along the edge of the moor. Branch left, to come out close to the starting point.

Walkerwood reservoir

WALK 6

BLEAKLOW FROM WILD BOAR CLOUGH

DIFFICULTY 🥾 🥾 🥾 🥾   **DISTANCE** 6½ miles (10.5 km)

TORSIDE — WILD BOAR CLOUGH — BLEAKLOW HEAD — TORSIDE CASTLE — PENNINE WAY — TORSIDE

MAP OS Explorer OL1, The Peak District – Dark Peak area

STARTING POINT Torside information centre, off the B6105 between Glossop and Woodhead (GR 068983)

PARKING Plenty of parking spaces at the information centre

PUBLIC TRANSPORT Currently the Holmfirth–Glossop bus service stops at Torside on Sundays and bank holidays only. Perhaps more usefully, National Express coaches between Liverpool/Manchester and Sheffield/Chesterfield make a stop at Crowden, about 1½ miles (2.5 km) away; there are up to three coaches each way daily.

Wild Boar Clough offers a wild and beautiful route up to the plateau of Bleaklow, with an easier – but equally attractive – route back down Torside Clough following the Pennine Way. Be prepared for some rough walking. Bleaklow is a notoriously easy place to lose your bearings, so you are advised to go prepared and to choose a day with good visibility.

▶ Walk up to the Longdendale Trail at the top of the Torside car park, and turn left.

■ The Longdendale Trail makes use of the former trans-Pennine railway line between Manchester and Sheffield. The line was originally built between 1839 and 1845, with the construction of the Woodhead tunnel (about 3 miles/4.8 km further to the east) the most challenging engineering work. A second tunnel was built shortly afterwards, and a new double tunnel built alongside a hundred years later, in 1949. At this stage, the Woodhead line was an important inter-city route. During the 1960s, however, British Railways decided to rationalize its trans-Pennine routes and the Woodhead was one of those marked for closure. Passenger services ended in 1970.

The Longdendale Trail is part of the Trans-Pennine Trail, a 215-mile (346-km) coast-to-coast route between Liverpool and Hull. More excitingly, perhaps, it also forms part of the European long-distance footpath E8. This route, it has been decided, is to begin in Ireland, at Dursey Head, west Cork, and to run through Killarney to Dublin. (Fortunately, walkers are allowed to catch the Dublin–Liverpool ferry, and the ferry from Hull to Rotterdam.) Once on the Continent, walkers can carry on through Holland to Germany, and then on to Austria, Slovakia and Hungary. Ultimately, the E8 will continue through Ukraine, Romania and Bulgaria to Istanbul (most of this latter part, it has to be said, is still at the planning stage). This sounds like just the thing for all those walkers who disdain mini-challenges like the Pennine Way.

▶ After only a hundred yards (100 m) or so ❶, turn right off the Longdendale Trail up a set of steps and over a stile, to find the path which heads up the hillside, to the right of Wild Boar Clough. (This path does not appear on OS maps.)

Continue, crossing over in due course so that the stream is on

© Crown Copyright 100043293 2004

your right. Above here, the
clough becomes rocky and
particularly impressive. The path
rapidly fades out, and the task
becomes one of scrambling over
the rocks up the side of the

clough. It's best to aim high,
rather than staying too close
to the water.

■ This section of Wild Boar
Clough is a delight, as the

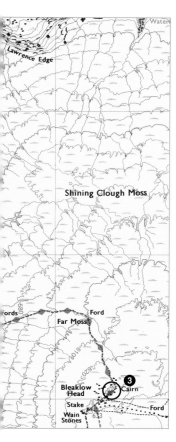

should meet up with a much better defined footpath coming in from the north-east. Take this path, and carry on up the side of the clough ❷.

■ Just to the west of Wild Boar Clough is another of the Dark Peak's aircraft crash sites. The remains of the RAF Bristol Blenheim which crashed here in the winter of 1939 still lie on the moor, marked by a cairn and small monument. The wreckage was found by a local walker.

▶ Continue up the side of Wild Boar Clough. When the stream and accompanying path turn sharply left, continue ahead over a stile, following a rather less defined track. This gradually disappears. The challenge now is to continue across the bleak peatlands of Shining Clough Moss, aiming for Bleaklow Head. It's easy to lose your way here, and a compass bearing is advisable. (The tendency can be to trend too far to the east, ending up in the wild ground to the east of both Bleaklow Head and the Pennine Way.)

water passes over a series of rocky ledges and small falls.

▶ After some minutes of scrambling, the clough side becomes less steep, and you

▶ page 74

'The Kiss': The Wain Stones, Bleaklow

■ Bleaklow Head ❸ at about 2060 ft (628 m) is the highest ground on the Bleaklow plateau, though the trig point is further south at Higher Shelf Stones. The Wain Stones near by were likened by Wainwright to a couple kissing.

▶ After more than 1 mile (1.6 km) of rough walking, it can be a relief to be on the Pennine Way. From Bleaklow Head, the Pennine Way runs north and then west, picking up the side of the stream called Wildboar Grain.

■ As the Pennine Way swings north again and crosses to the left bank of the stream, it's worth making the detour to Torside Castle ❹. This is a striking mound, covered in grass, which rises above the heather hillside. For a long time it was assumed to be a prehistoric man-made site of some kind, although it now seems possible that the mound may be natural.

Torside Castle has attracted more than its share of supernatural stories. The *Fortean Times* magazine, for example, has claimed that mysterious phantom lights have been seen flickering near by. Longdendale itself is claimed by some UFO researchers to be a particular hotspot for alien activity.

▶ From Torside Castle, it's possible to continue across the moor to pick up the Pennine Way again towards the bottom of Torside Clough. However, the route taken by the Pennine Way in descending the clough offers such a spectacular walk, as the path winds high up above the rocky sides of the valley, that it's probably better to retrace your steps.

Follow the Pennine Way ❺ right down to the B road, and then take the Longdendale Trail back to Torside.

WALK 7

LADDOW ROCKS

DIFFICULTY 🥾 🥾 🥾 🥾   **DISTANCE** 6½ miles (10.5 km)

CROWDEN — LAD'S LEAP — ANONYMOUS TRIG (RAKES MOSS) — CHEW CLOUGH — LADDOW ROCKS — CROWDEN

MAP OS Explorer OL1, The Peak District – Dark Peak area

STARTING POINT Crowden (between Tintwistle and Woodhead, on the A628)

PARKING Crowden visitors' car park (GR 072993)

PUBLIC TRANSPORT National Express coaches between Liverpool/Manchester and Sheffield/Chesterfield make a stop at Crowden. There are up to three coaches each way daily. A Sunday and bank holiday bus service between Holmfirth and Glossop stops within ½ mile (0.8 km) of the walk start.

A short but challenging walk into the empty spaces of the peat moors north of Longdendale. Best undertaken in good weather conditions.

■ The Longdendale valley was transformed during the mid-nineteenth century, as Manchester's growing requirement for unpolluted drinking water led to the construction of a string of reservoirs along the valley. Torside reservoir, south of Crowden, was completed in 1864. Woodhead reservoir to the east was begun in 1848, but problems with leaks in the embankment meant that

© Crown Copyright 100043293 2004

it took almost thirty years to complete.

The building of the reservoirs led to the loss of farmland in the valley bottom and to the compulsory purchase of many of the upland farms. Crowden, once a sizeable community, shrank to just a few houses. However Crowden does have its youth hostel, famously providing the first (or last) night's accommodation for those walking the Pennine Way.

▶ From the Crowden car park, turn right by the toilet block, walk to the entrance of the campsite and there turn left, following signs to the Pennine Way. Cross Crowden Brook and almost immediately turn right on to the Pennine Way ❶, heading north. After a few hundred yards (metres), at the edge of open country and beside a small copse of trees ❷, turn left on to a path which heads up the side of a hill.

After the first short climb and beside a broken-down wall, turn left. This path climbs further, initially towards Highstone Rocks before turning slightly to head off to the north-west. There are fine views back across Longdendale to Bleaklow.

After about ¾ mile (just over 1 km), the path drops down to the waterfalls at Lad's Leap ❸. At this point, it's necessary to leave the path to venture across the peaty and boggy ground of Rakes Moss to the trig point at GR 046012 (spot height 541 m).

This is rough going. If you are lucky, you may pick up the occasional trod (faint path); if not, be prepared to cope with peat groughs (channels) and haggs (banks). In choosing the route, stay close to the line of Hollins Clough, which drains almost from the trig point itself. Since the trig point is on the watershed, you know that as long as the water is still flowing south you are on the right route! ❹

■ No doubt somebody has a name for this trig point, but the OS map has none to offer. Using the authorial power with which he is invested, this writer suggests 'Anonymous trig' – anything grander would surely be inappropriate to the surroundings. This must be the loneliest trig point in the Peak.

Looking up Crowden Great Brook to Laddow Rocks

▶ Continue beyond the trig point, this time picking up one of the peaty channels which run northwards from the trig point into Chew Clough. The water of Chew reservoir should soon come into sight to the left. At the bottom ❺, a real footpath complete with cairns is finally reached. Turn right here and follow the path back up to the watershed and then down to Laddow Rocks ❻.

■ Laddow Rocks occupy an important place in the history of climbing in Britain. Rock climbing in the Peak began in the late nineteenth century, and the gritstone crags were the first to be explored. Laddow became a firm favourite not least because access to the rocks was tolerated. A number of routes up the crags were put up in these early years.

It was a climbing accident at Laddow which led to the first steps towards proper mountain rescue in the north of England. After an injured climber had been taken off the hills strapped to a

five-bar gate, the Rucksack Club and the Fell and Rock Club came together in 1933 to establish the Joint Stretcher Committee, which set to work to design an appropriate stretcher for mountain-rescue use. The actual design was undertaken by Eustace Thomas. An early fell walker and alpinist then in his sixties, he had started the tradition of epic Lakeland rounds in 1922 when he tackled sixty-six peaks and 25,500 ft (7775 m) of climbing within twenty-four hours. The 'Thomas stretcher' entered service in 1935. The Joint Stretcher Committee was the forerunner of the Mountain Rescue Committee.

There is a cave below the overhang at the north end of the outcrop.

▶ From Laddow Rocks, it is an easy walk back to Crowden, following the route of the Pennine Way down the hillside. The heather slopes of little Oakenclough Brook, just south of Laddow, are a particular delight.

The Holme Moss
fell race

London may have its marathon every year, but when it comes to long tough days out for runners the north of England has its own speciality to offer: fell racing.

The Cumbrian fells are home to some classic British mountain races, including long-established events like Borrowdale and Ennerdale. But the Peak District and south Pennines areas also have a strong fell-running tradition, and the annual Holme Moss fell race is an opportunity for runners to get to grips with the particular challenges of Pennine millstone grit country.

The Holme Moss fell race has been run since the late 1980s and is the brain-child of Russell Bangham, who has been organizing it each year since then on behalf of his local running club, the Holmfirth Harriers. 'I wanted to create a really, really tough fell race around here. I think I got pretty close,' he says.

The Fellrunners' Association classifies the race as AL, the highest classification, meaning that it is both long in distance and involves a considerable amount of climbing – about sixteen miles (twenty-six kilometres) and 4000 ft (1220 m), in fact. From the start next to Brownhill reservoir near Holme, the route includes Ramsden moor, Crowden and Black Hill, taking in much of the territory covered in this book in Walk 8 and Walk 9. But the fell race specifically seeks out opportunities for extra climbing, including an ascent of Ramsden Clough, another up the side of Heyden Brook south of the television mast and a final gruelling hands-and-knees climb up the side of the Laddow Rocks from the valley below.

Despite this, the best fell runners can get round the course in not much more than two hours. The record, in fact, is just five seconds over two hours, set in 1996 by champion fell runner Ian

Holmes (the best time for a woman runner is two hours and thirty-three minutes). Anyone tempted to compete and fancying their chances should know that since 1996 Russell Bangham has offered a £150 prize to the first runner who can beat the two-hour mark for the race.

Russell Bangham himself has recently developed knee problems and has had to hang up his fell-running shoes,

consoling himself instead with mountain biking. But, at least for the time being, the Holme Moss fell race carries on. Each year on a Sunday in July, whatever the weather, volunteers are out on the hilltops staffing the checkpoints, offering drinks and providing first aid. And every year a hundred or so runners line up at the start to make their best effort, racing their way across the Pennine moors.

The trig point on Black Hill, visited in the Holme Moss fell race

WALK 8

CROWDEN LITTLE BROOK

DIFFICULTY 🥾 🥾 🥾   **DISTANCE** 6 miles (9.6 km)

CROWDEN   CROWDEN LITTLE BROOK   MEADOW CLOUGH   BAREHOLME MOSS   CROWDEN

MAP OS Explorer OL1, The Peak District – Dark Peak area

STARTING POINT Crowden (between Tintwistle and Woodhead, on the A628)

PARKING Crowden visitors' car park (GR 072993)

PUBLIC TRANSPORT National Express coaches between Liverpool/Manchester and Sheffield/Chesterfield make a stop at Crowden. There are up to three coaches each way daily. A Sunday and bank holiday bus service between Holmfirth and Glossop stops within ½ mile (0.8 km) of the walk start.

A circuit of the moors south of Black Hill, following the Crowden Little Brook and Crowden Great Brook valleys. Some rough walking in open country.

▶ From the Crowden car park, turn right by the toilet block, pass the entrance of the campsite and continue ahead. Very shortly, take a right fork on to a track, and then – again very shortly – leave this track to the right, following a sign with the enticing invitation 'to open country' ❶.

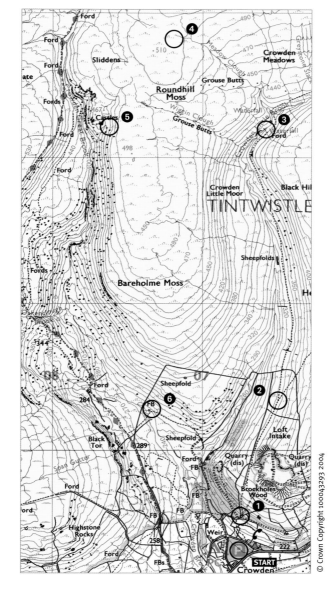

■ The route of the Pennine Way from Crowden at one stage came this way, running over Hey Moss and Tooleyshaw Moor and then heading north-westwards to Black Hill. The route now runs further to the west, using the valley of Crowden Great Brook and passing Laddow Rocks. Since much of that section has been extensively paved, we must assume that this will continue to be the definitive route. The Tooleyshaw alternative remains, however, as a quieter (and wetter) choice.

▶ When the path reaches the edge of extensive quarry workings, look for the left fork ❷ which will take you along the side of Crowden Little Brook. The path, or more precisely a grassy track, is easy to follow as it runs on, into the heart of the valley.

Eventually the track shrinks into a footpath. Continue until you are opposite the entrance to Meadow Clough (the first prominent clough coming in to Crowden Little Brook from the left) ❸. Here cross the stream, and scramble up the side of the waterfall at the bottom of Meadow Clough. (The left side of the fall is probably the better choice.)

Immediately, a second, slightly smaller waterfall becomes visible. Clamber up the side of this as well.

■ These falls, while they may not be the most dramatic in Britain, are still worth a visit – or at least this is certainly the view of author Griff Fellows, who includes them in his guide *The Waterfalls of England*. The heather banks and rocks provide a particularly pleasing frame for the lower falls.

▶ At the top of the higher falls, on the further (northern) side of the stream, you can pick up a relatively well-walked path. This runs north-westwards across the moor, a little to the right of the upper waters of Meadow Clough.

The path makes a line for the only landmark in this area of moorland, the wreckage of two

RAF Meteors which crashed here in 1951 ❹. Despite the fact that more than half a century has gone by, the wreckage of the planes remains extensive and is strewn over a considerable area of ground.

■ The full story of the training exercise in poor weather conditions, which took place on 12 April 1951 and which ended in tragedy for the pilots of the two Meteors, is told in Ron Collier and Roni Wilkinson's book *Dark Peak Aircraft Wrecks 1*. Four Meteors were involved in the exercise to simulate an air battle. It seems probable that the two planes which crashed had simply lost their bearings in the cloud cover; Collier and Wilkinson suggest that one of the pilots, who radioed that he had seen Leeds when the clouds momentarily parted, had probably sighted Stockport instead.

A small wooden cross, bearing the names of the two pilots who died, has been positioned close to some of the more prominent wreckage.

▶ The path continues past further plane wreckage, before dropping over the hilltop and down into the Crowden Great Brook valley.

From here, make your way south along the brow of the hillside, passing the impressive rock outcrops (marked on OS maps as Castles) to your right ❺. You will be able to pick up a succession of sheep tracks, though some rough walking is likely to be necessary.

■ Across the valley are the impressive Laddow Rocks, visited in the previous walk (for details of the place of the Laddow Rocks in early British climbing history, see page 80).

▶ Continue walking along the side of Bareholme Moss. Occasionally old tree trunks can be seen, emerging out of the peat, relics of the time when this landscape was much more heavily forested.

▶ page 90

The valley at Crowden

In due course, Crowden will come into sight at the foot of the valley. It's now a question of scrambling down the steep side of the valley, choosing the best line possible through the heather and bracken. Aim for the small metal footbridge ❻ marked on OS maps at GR 066003 (though don't cross the bridge). From here, follow the path east and then south, to emerge at the base of Brockholes Wood.

■ Brockholes Wood is one of the few remaining areas of natural woodland in the Crowden valley, and is now a nature reserve. A board beside the path gives further information.

▶ Return to Crowden car park, to complete the walk.

Holme Moss
television transmitter

It was the Holme Moss transmitter, now a familiar landmark on the south Pennine moors, which was responsible for bringing television to the north of England.

In the years immediately after the Second World War, the BBC began rolling out its embryonic television service to the nation. Before the war, only 20,000 people owned television sets, but afterwards the numbers rose quickly, to more than a million by 1951. It was time to ensure that all the country, not just the Home Counties, could enjoy the dawning age of television.

Sutton Coldfield near Birmingham provided the location for the necessary mast for the Midlands area, and from there the BBC engineers turned their attention to the north. Holme Moss, more than 1700 ft (520 m) up on the bleak open moorland near Black Hill, was where they found themselves heading.

Work began on the site in January 1950, initially with the focus on infrastructure. A tunnel of earthenware pipes had to be laid down to the Woodhead road two miles (three kilometres) away, where the existing GPO telephone network could be reached, and another two-mile (three-kilometre) run of pipes to Holme village was put in to cope with sewage disposal from the site. Press reports of the time talk of this work being undertaken in 'driving rain and a blustering wind'.

By March the focus had moved on to the new approach road to the transmitter site, and this too was slow progress. The *Huddersfield Examiner* reported, with perhaps just a note of smugness, that 'The moor at that spot is composed of peaty soil which does not readily yield to the bull-dozers and shovels.'

Eventually the road was completed and enough peat stripped away from the moor to provide space for the reinforced concrete foundations of the mast itself. When built, the mast reached 750 ft (230 m) into the Yorkshire sky, with the whole edifice balanced on a two-inch (five-centimetre) steel ball designed to allow a little movement in high winds – a necessary consideration, given the gales which can howl over Black Hill.

The BBC proudly launched their television service from Holme Moss in October 1951 with a special programme broadcast from Manchester; studio guests included northern folk heroes Gracie Fields and Stanley Matthews. The technical arrangements were complicated: pictures and sound arrived at Holme Moss separately, the vision signals via coaxial cable from Manchester and the sound through high-quality telephone lines supplied by the GPO. But once the programmes found their way to Holme Moss, a population of thirteen million could be reached. The coverage area extended far beyond Yorkshire and Lancashire, with the signal reaching down to the Wash, up to what was then Cumberland and across to north Wales.

Since those early days, Holme Moss has continued to provide television (and later radio) to the north of England, being joined later in the 1950s by transmitters on other sites erected for independent television.

But along the way there have been moments of some anxiety. The complete collapse of the independent-television mast at Emley Moor in 1969, under the weight of ice, led to considerable concern about safety at other transmitter sites. Holme Moss had to evacuate its staff for a period of weeks in particularly bad weather in the 1980s, after massive chunks of ice fell hundreds of feet and smashed four holes in the reinforced concrete roof of the station.

The original Holme Moss mast lasted for about thirty years, after which it was replaced by the current mast. For a very short time, in fact, the hilltop sported two almost identical masts, side by side, before the 1950s pioneer was carefully dismantled.

WALK 9

HOLME MOSS AND RAMSDEN CLOUGH

DIFFICULTY 🥾 🥾 🥾 🥾   **DISTANCE** 11½ miles (18.4 km)

HOLME   BILBERRY   NETHER   BLACK   HOLME   BRITLAND   RAMSDEN   RAMSDEN   HOLME
   RESERVOIR   LANE   HILL   MOSS   EDGE HILL   CLOUGH   RESERVOIR

MAP OS Explorer OL1, The Peak District – Dark Peak area

STARTING POINT Holme village (GR 108059)

PARKING Limited parking in the centre of Holme village

PUBLIC TRANSPORT Buses run from Huddersfield and Holmfirth.

One of the toughest, but also one of the finest, walks in the book. A reminder of how wild, and how beautiful, this part of the Peak District National Park can be.

▶ From Holme, walk up Meal Hill Road, turning almost immediately right on to a footpath (marked with a painted 'K', denoting the route of the Kirklees Way). Follow this pleasant field footpath down to the dam between Bilberry and Digley reservoirs ❶.

■ Bilberry reservoir is a peaceful place today with little to suggest the devastation which was caused in 1852 when it burst its dam, creating the worst flood ever experienced by Holmfirth and the Holme valley, and resulting in the loss of eighty-one lives (see pages 102–4).

Its near neighbour, Digley reservoir, is a more recent addition to the landscape, having been completed in 1954.

▶ Continue beyond the reservoirs along the Kirklees Way, as it turns to run westwards along Nether Lane. There are good views up to the left, to Black Hill and the Holme Moss television transmitter.

It's possible to continue along this farm track to the top of Reap Head Clough, and there to pick up the Pennine Way. Another, and perhaps more pleasant,

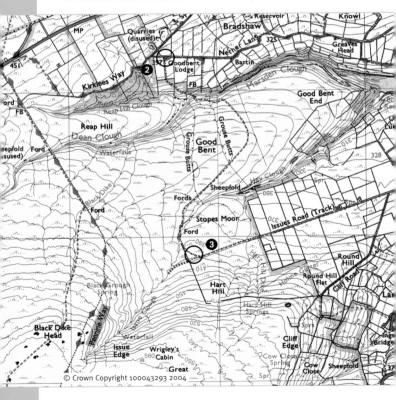

option however is to turn left beyond Goodbent Lodge farmhouse ❷ on to the footpath which meanders across Good Bent and Stopes Moor. This path drops down to cross Marsden Clough beside a set of small waterfalls, and then makes its way across the heather.

As the path turns to meet up with the track known as Issues Road, turn back right ❸ and take the shooting track which emerges from the end of Issues Road. Continue heading along this track as it crosses Issue Clough stream and starts climbing the hillside. In a short

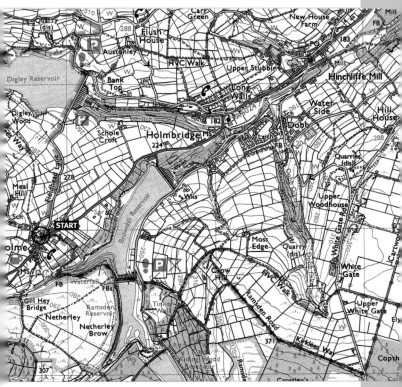

▶ Map continues southwards on pages 96–7

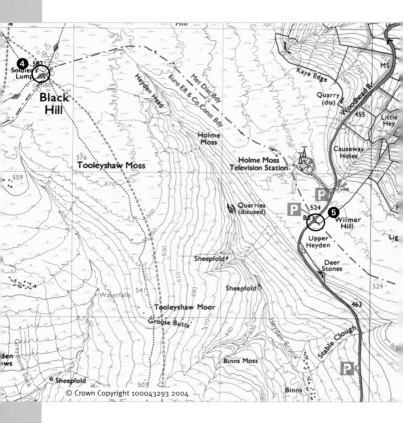

© Crown Copyright 100043293 2004

while, as the shooting track turns back to the right, pick up the well-walked footpath which runs up the hillside. The footpath becomes paved and soon meets up with the Pennine Way. Here turn left, and continue on to Black Hill ❹.

■ Black Hill, at 1908 ft (582 m), had a fearsome reputation among early travellers on the Pennine Way. Arthur Wainwright in his *Pennine Way Companion* described the approach as a 'wet and weary trudge', and went on:

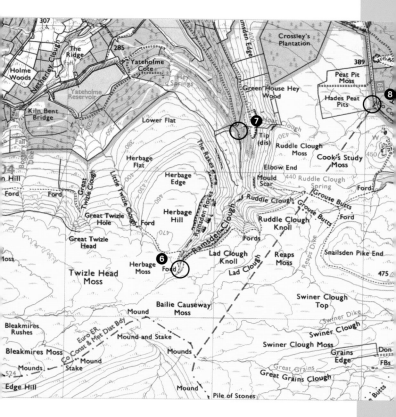

Black Hill is well named.
The broad top really *is*
black. It is not the only
fell with a summit of peat,
but no other shows such
a desolate and hopeless
quagmire to the sky.
This is peat naked and

unashamed. Nature
fashioned it, but for once
has no suggestion for
clothing it.

Wainwright also wanted to
warn unwary walkers: 'It is a
frightening place in bad

weather, a dangerous place after heavy rain. It is NOT a place to visit unaccompanied, especially after prolonged rainy weather, because of the risk of becoming trapped or even entombed in the seepage hollows.'

Since Wainwright's day, the whole of the Pennine Way route across Black Hill has been paved, and the experience is not quite so daunting. Nevertheless, Black Hill continues to be a place which seems to attract terrible weather.

▶ Unfortunately, the route from Black Hill involves leaving the comfort of the paved Pennine Way to head across the peat haggs (banks) and groughs (channels) to the television mast at Holme Moss. It's a question of picking your way with care to avoid the worst of the bogs. Rather than aiming directly for the television mast, which involves dropping into Heyden Clough and climbing out the other side, initially walk roughly due east before turning south-eastwards towards the mast.

If the clag (hill cloud) is down, a compass bearing will be essential at this point.

■ Holme Moss television mast was opened in October 1951 and brought television for the first time to a large part of the north of England. The original mast was replaced in the 1980s, after fears that it could collapse –

a fate which befell nearby Emley Moor television transmitter in 1969 (see pages 91–2).

▶ From the border fence around the transmitter station, make for the A6024 Holme Moss road, crossing it at the brow, at the Yorkshire/Derbyshire border ❺. Continue over the road on to the moors opposite. The next target is the top of Ramsden Clough, well over a mile (about 2 km) away to the east. One option is to bash on over the open moorland, across Lightens Edge and Great Twizle Head. A slightly easier, if longer, alternative is to follow the wire fence which marks the Yorkshire/Derbyshire border. Although wet in places, there are no difficulties of navigation to contend with. Follow the fence

Holme valley

south round Britland Edge Hill and then back round to the north-east. At this point, cross the fence at an appropriate point and head north. Initially, this seems unpromising ground. Quickly, however, the very top of Ramsden Clough is reached ❻.

■ Ramsden Clough is a strikingly beautiful and wild valley, enclosed by rocky outcrops high up on both sides above the river. It has deservedly been called one of the gems of the Peak District. For many years, however, Ramsden was very definitely private property and the public were kept firmly out.

This rankled with older residents in the Holme valley whose memories went back to a time when access had been tolerated and Ramsden Clough had been the local beauty spot which many had grown to love. The effective closure of this part of the moors made it feel as though an invisible border had been put in place, across which passage was impossible.

While still a private shooting estate, Ramsden Clough is now once more, thanks to the new access legislation, a place which all can enjoy. At this point, we momentarily meet up with our companion Freedom to Roam guide, *Peak District: Eastern Moors and the South*, which offers an approach to Ramsden Clough from the south.

▶ Follow Ramsden Clough down river. (The shorter route is to keep to the left-hand hillside.) At the bottom, clamber down the steep hill to the side of the river ❼. From here, the obvious route back is by means of the track through the woodlands which border Riding Wood reservoir. Unfortunately, however, the new access legislation does not extend to woodland and at the time of writing it was not clear whether a separate access agreement would be negotiated to permit use of this route home.

If access through the woods has subsequently been agreed, this will be clear from OS maps and on the ground. Otherwise, the route has to stay on open country and this unfortunately means a stiff clamber up the further side of Ramsden Clough, aiming for the edge of Crossley's Plantation at the top. From here, cross the moorland eastwards, to join the minor road close to spot height 389 m ❽.

Take the rough track known as Ramsden Road back north-westwards, to emerge finally beside the water of Ramsden reservoir. The Kirklees Way follows Ramsden Road, and in places painted 'K' signs are visible again.

Cross the dam between Ramsden and Brownhill reservoirs, following the Kirklees Way back to the village of Holme.

Bradshaw, near Holme

The great Holmfirth flood

When it rains on the south Pennine hills, the rivers which carry rainwater off the moors rise in height. When it rains very heavily, the water levels can rise very rapidly. And just occasionally, in exceptional weather conditions, the quantity of rainwater which has to be carried away by the rivers is simply too much, and flooding is the result.

For Holmfirth, at the confluence of several rivers, flooding has regrettably been a feature of the town's history on a number of occasions. In 1738 a severe thunderstorm and cloudburst in May resulted in floodwater rushing down the Ribble valley into the town. It was a similar tale in July 1777, when a 'most awful thunderstorm' over the hills above the town resulted in a flash flood which claimed three lives. Within living memory, on Whit Monday in May 1944, yet another torrential rainstorm and cloudburst at the head of the valley led to an estimated one-and-a-half million tons of water pouring down the Holme valley, through Holmbridge and Holmfirth and on towards Honley and beyond. There was much damage to property and to cars, and as in 1777 three people were killed.

Holmfirth's worst-ever flood, however, was caused not by freak weather conditions but simply by gross human negligence. At 1am on Thursday 5 February 1852, the dam of Bilberry reservoir gave way. It was, it has been said, 'one of the direst calamities upon record'. The water from the reservoir high up above Holmfirth emptied itself straight into the valley, creating a wave of water many feet high. There was a terrible loss of property and of life: eighty-one people killed. And it was entirely avoidable. Indeed, many local people knew that the reservoir dam was unsafe and had predicted the flood.

Bilberry reservoir was built not to provide drinking water but in order to ensure a dependable supply of water to power the mills of the Holme valley. The plans for the reservoir were approved in 1837 by Parliament, and the Holme Reservoir Commissioners (mainly local mill owners) were established to finance the project and oversee the work.

Right from the start, things began to go wrong. The dam started leaking and the top of the embankment slipped, so that it was lower than one of the bye-wash channels constructed as a safety feature to drain away excess water. The commissioners fell out with the original contractors, who were replaced before the work was completed. The chief engineer was hardly ever on site. And the whole project ran into major financial problems, so that the money was not available to pay for the remedial work which was needed.

By the end of the 1840s, almost the whole Holme valley knew that there were problems at Bilberry. Then in 1852, in early February, heavy and continuous rain began falling in the area. Over two inches (five centimetres) of rain fell in one twenty-four-hour period and the water ran off the moors straight into the reservoir, which began to be dangerously full. Attempts were made to let out some of the surplus water, but yet again there were technical problems: one of the key valves was found not to be working.

By early evening on 4 February, the water was within eight feet (two and a half metres) of the top of the dam. By midnight, it was level with the top and the water began to pour over. By 1am the dam had given way.

A number of local people, aware of the risks, had been out at Bilberry monitoring the situation. However, things happened so fast that they were unable to raise the alarm. The floodwater swept down the valley below the reservoir, taking with it major local landmarks: Bilberry Mill (partly destroyed), Bilberry Bridge (swept away), Upper Digley Mill (gutted), Digley Mill (gutted, thirty-four power looms carried away), Bank End Mill (wrecked, machinery carried off) and so on to the first major settlement, Holmbridge. Here the church was flooded to a height of about five feet (one and a half metres) and many of the weavers' cottages destroyed. One eye-witness later described how a terrace of six houses had 'wobbled' before being carried off in the floodwater.

Holmfirth, too, was the scene of terrible destruction, with shops, houses, pubs and mills destroyed or seriously damaged. There were, however, tales of remarkable escapes. One man named George Crosland described afterwards how he was saved as water invaded his house by managing to hold on to a sampler which had been hung in a frame on the wall; fortunately the nail into the wall held firm.

There was suffering, however, even for those who had been fortunate enough to survive the flood. Over seven thousand people found themselves jobless, their livelihoods destroyed at the same time as the mills in which they had worked.

The judgment of the coroner's court jury afterwards was unequivocal: 'that the Bilberry reservoir was defective in its original construction, and that the commissioners, the engineer, and the overlooker were greatly culpable in not seeing to the proper regulation of the works'. But those responsible could not be brought to book. As the jury put it: 'We regret that, the reservoir being under the management of a corporation, prevents us bringing in a verdict of manslaughter, as we are convinced that the gross and culpable negligence of the commissioners would have subjected them to such a verdict had they been in the position of an individual or a firm.'

Bilberry reservoir was subsequently repaired, helped by £7,000 taken from donations sent by well-wishers to the Holme valley after the disaster.

WALK 10

MELTHAM MOOR

DIFFICULTY   **DISTANCE** 7¾ miles (12.5 km)

MELTHAM   WEST NAB   RAVEN ROCKS   DEER HILL CONDUIT   DEER HILL RESERVOIR   MELTHAM

MAPS OS Explorer OL21, South Pennines; OS Explorer OL1, The Peak District – Dark Peak area

STARTING POINT Meltham village (GR 100107)

PARKING In one of Meltham's side-streets

PUBLIC TRANSPORT Buses run from Huddersfield, and from Holmfirth and Marsden.

A fine circumnavigation of Meltham Moor, with plenty of good views to enjoy. Easy walking for the most part, but with about ½ mile (0.8 km) of (unavoidable) rough moorland to cross.

▶ From the centre of Meltham, walk a short way along the Holmfirth road, turning right opposite the primary school into Calmlands Road **1**. When the road stops, continue ahead along a track, enjoying the views down to Royd Edge Clough to the left as you walk.

At a gate, when the track continues downhill towards old quarries, take the footpath which carries on almost straight ahead, following the left-hand side of a wall. Keep to this footpath until Wessenden Head Road is reached at High Moor **2**. It's worth turning round periodically to enjoy the view.

▶ page 110

THE NATIONAL TRUST

MARSDEN
MOOR ESTATE

THE NATIONAL TRUST

OPEN TO THE PUBLIC
(SUBJECT TO THE BYELAWS
ON THE BACK OF THIS NOTICE)

PLEASE AVOID
LEAVING LITTER
LIGHTING FIRES
DAMAGING TREES
OR PLANTS

Wessenden valley

START

109

■ Emley Moor television mast, at 1083 ft (330 m) the tallest self-supporting mast in Britain, dominates the skyline. The steel lattice mast is supported by a 900-ft (275-m) concrete section with an observation platform (reached by a lift) at the top. The current structure replaces the former Emley Moor mast which collapsed on 19 March 1969 as a result of icing.

Closer to hand is another local landmark, the Victoria Tower on Castle Hill near Huddersfield. The tower was built in 1899 to mark Queen Victoria's sixty years on the throne. Castle Hill itself is a Bronze Age hill fort.

▶ Walk for a short way along Wessenden Head Road, before turning right on to the signed concessionary path which quickly climbs up the stony outcrop known as West Nab Brow, to reach the trig point at West Nab itself ❸. Just before the trig point, a circular construction offers shelter from the winds.

From here continue past another small outcrop, the Rocking Stone, to reach the Raven Rocks ❹. Beyond, cross the wire fence and head across the tussocky open moorland of Holly Bank Moss. This is quite hard going. Either aim for the top of Little Hey Sike Clough or for neighbouring Great Hey Sike Clough slightly to the right.

Whichever clough you choose to follow, halfway down a path comes in from the south-east. Turn right on to this path, and continue as it contours up the hillside above the Wessenden valley. Great Hey Sike Clough is crossed by a small wooden bridge beside an impressive waterfall ❺.

■ The Wessenden reservoir was originally dammed in the late eighteenth century to ensure an adequate supply of water to power the woollen mills below. In the later nineteenth century, Huddersfield corporation took it over to supply drinking water for the town and neighbouring areas, adding the three other reservoirs which occupy the valley today.

On the further side of Wessenden reservoir, the

Pennine Way can be seen coming in from the west.

▶ Continue on the same hillside path, which in due course begins to run alongside a reedy disused water conduit (these are known locally as catchwater drains). Pule Hill and the outskirts of Marsden come into view.

Above Marsden, the path and catchwater drain both turn abruptly north-east ❻ and the drain becomes full, taking water from the Wessenden valley to Deer Hill reservoir above Meltham. Eventually, the path fetches up beside a rifle range ❼.

■ It is because of this rifle range that a large part of Meltham Moor, although open country, has been excluded from the access provisions of the Countryside and Rights of Way Act. Most of Deer Hill Moss south of Shooter's Nab and north of the Raven Rocks has been closed, in case of overshooting from the range.

This exclusion order, made in 2004, was contested by local members of the Ramblers' Association. They pointed out that stray bullets from the range would have to make their way up the almost vertical face of Shooter's Nab, at least 100 ft (30 m) high. Anyone firing bullets on to the excluded area of Deer Hill Moss, therefore, would have to be an almost unbelievably bad shot. Unfortunately, their argument failed to convince the authorities. (All restrictions are reviewed at least every five years, however, so there is a possibility that this one may be removed in the future.)

▶ Walk along Deer Hill reservoir, dropping from the embankment at the north-east corner to pick up the field footpath across White Reaps to Deer Hill End ❽. From here, take the bridleway running south-east round the side of Deer Hill. Turn left, and either follow Red Lane back to Meltham or – more pleasant – turn right on to another catchwater drain which contours round the western end of Meltham, leaving the drain to return to Meltham on the Wessenden Head Road.

Royd Edge, near Meltham

'Hiking' the Standedge tunnel

To get to know the Pennines really up-close and intimate, there's not much to beat the experience of walking the hills and moors. But there is one other way and that's 600 ft (180 m) down, actually inside the Pennines.

The Standedge tunnel between Marsden in the east and Diggle in the west has its place in the record books as the highest, longest and deepest canal tunnel in the country. By any sensible commercial logic, it shouldn't exist: the Huddersfield Narrow Canal company, which took seventeen years to get the tunnel completed, was never really a commercial proposition. It was in financial crisis for much of its early life and only occasionally managed to pay its shareholders a dividend. (The company was eventually saved from financial collapse only because the local Huddersfield–Manchester railway decided to buy it out.)

This same commercial logic would certainly decree that the Standedge canal tunnel should today be derelict, unsafe and boarded up. After all, not many years ago the whole twenty miles (thirty kilometres) or so of the Huddersfield Narrow Canal was unusable. Locks had been filled with concrete, the canal itself culverted in many places, and several factories (and much of Stalybridge town centre) had been built over the top of the old route. The legal right to navigation had been extinguished. This was in every sense an ex-canal.

And yet, amazingly, miraculously, triumphantly, the whole Huddersfield Narrow Canal is today once more open for boats. The story of how a band of enthusiastic volunteers in the Inland Waterways Association and the Huddersfield Canal Society began to create the momentum which ultimately persuaded the authorities to invest the millions needed to reopen the canal has been told from the inside by Keith Gibson, in his fascinating account *Pennine Dreams*. This was, as he says, as much a story of an unlikely dream fulfilled as was the original construction of the canal back in the years after 1793.

With the reopening of the Huddersfield Narrow Canal on 1 May 2001 came the chance once again to savour at first hand the experience of a transit of the Standedge tunnel. British Waterways won't allow the public to guide their own boats through the tunnel, but about three times a week they arrange for those vessels wanting to cross to be linked together behind an electric tug and towed through. Even better, when there is space they make a few extra tickets available for people who just want to go for the ride. British Waterways calls these its 'hikers' tickets', and they represent one of the best-value and most unusual visitor attractions in the North.

The tunnel is three and a quarter miles long (about five kilometres), and the journey through takes, on a good day, about two and a half hours. In other words, the pace of travel is a touch more than a mile an hour. On a bad day, it takes longer. Sometimes, for example, boats in the convoy get stuck. Even though the water level in the tunnel was dropped by about six inches (fifteen centimetres) when the tunnel was reopened, specifically to help modern boats obtain the clearance they need, Standedge can still be a tight squeeze. The convoy of boats (normally no more than five) is like a fish which has to squirm and wriggle its way through the tight spots – staff at British Waterways have learned not to put the lightest boat at the rear because it will tend to act like a tail, thrashing about from side to side. British Waterways also has to position a member of staff on each boat in the convoy, ready to fend off from the tunnel sides.

Some days, there are other problems. It has been known, for example, for passengers to be overcome with claustrophobia, and to require evacuation. It is also not unknown for the electric tug to break down, and for the convoy to have to wait in the tunnel for a relief tug to pull it out.

Standedge was built with enormous difficulty. It was constructed partly from either end and partly from a series of shafts sunk from the top of the hill above. The navvies in the shafts drilled holes, packed them with gunpowder, lit the fuses and then clung on for dear life to a rope which they hoped would winch them a safe distance above the chaos below. The work was undertaken by candlelight.

Not surprisingly, given the construction method, the tunnel didn't end up completely straight. In fact, there was a discrepancy of as much as twenty-six feet (about eight metres) in the middle. This means that the Standedge tunnel convoys have to negotiate an S-bend halfway through, adding to the difficulty of the navigational task. There are other hazards, too, such as cascades of water from the tunnel ceiling which periodically drench unwary passengers on the observation platforms – or what British Waterways wits like to describe as the 'sun decks' – at either end of the main passenger boat.

Standedge canal tunnel was completed in 1811. Less than forty years later, between 1846 and 1849, it was joined by a single-track railway tunnel, constructed a little above the canal and just to the south. Between 1868 and 1870 came a second railway tunnel, alongside the first. Finally, between 1890 and 1894, the double-track tunnel still used by trains today was built, also above canal level and slightly to the north of the canal tunnel. If you take a British Waterways transit through Standedge, you will know when a train is passing close by, not only from the noise and vibration it causes but also from the thin mist which momentarily descends on the canal, the result of a change in atmospheric pressure. There is also just one point where it's possible to look from the canal into the active railway tunnel and catch a glimpse of passing trains, ghost-like above.

Even for people not inclined to claustrophobia, it can be a relief eventually to emerge into daylight at the tunnel ends at Marsden or Diggle. But in the old days of the Huddersfield Narrow Canal, getting through Standedge was an altogether tougher experience: those were the days when barges had to be 'legged' through by boatmen lying on their backs on the barge roofs. The record for legging a barge through Standedge, so it's said, was one hour and twenty-five minutes, though it should also be added that British Waterways staff today don't see how one man could have made it in that sort of time. Frankly, however much you enjoy walking, Standedge tunnel is one place where it's good to rely on electricity, and just be grateful that your feet can have a rest.

Inside Standedge tunnel

Samuel Laycock

Samuel Laycock was to achieve fame – if not exactly fortune – within Lancashire as one of the county's best-loved poets, writing primarily in the dialect he heard spoken all around him.

He was born in 1824. His father was a handloom weaver, a traditional but at that time dying occupation, and the family lived initially on the Yorkshire side of the Pennines, at Intake Head Farm just up the hill from Marsden Tunnel End (Walk 11 will take you close). Samuel himself began working in the woollen mills locally when he was nine, labouring from six in the morning to eight at night in exchange for a wage of two shillings a week.

Then, when he was eleven, his family made the move across the Pennines from Yorkshire to Lancashire, settling in the town of Stalybridge. Samuel spent his days as a power-loom weaver in the cotton mills there but, like so many other working-class people of that time, he was also deeply committed to the great goal of self-improvement and both read widely and developed his own writing.

Ironically, Laycock first received popular acclaim as a poet as a result of a major crisis. During the American Civil War of the early 1860s, raw cotton was unable to get through to Britain from the southern states, and the weaving mills ground to a halt. These were the Famine Years in Lancashire, and Laycock's *Famine Songs* were written and published during this time.

Many of his songs were published as broadsheets, and learned by heart. There was one song in particular which immediately became popular. This was 'Welcome, Bonny Brid'. It is a verse composed by a father to his new-born

Samuel Laycock

118

baby, welcoming the child into an uncertain and difficult world. The first two stanzas are as follows (for those in need of some assistance, 'brid' is bird and 'pobbies' a term for milk and bread, the sort of soft food suitable for a child's diet):

Tha'rt welcome, little bonny brid,
But shouldn't ha' come just when tha did;
Toimes are bad.
We're short o' pobbies for eawr Joe,
But that, of course, tha didn't know
Did ta, lad?

Aw've often yeard mi feyther tell,
'At when aw coom i'th' world misel'
Trade wur slack;
And neaw its hard work pooin' throo –
But aw munno fear thee, – iv aw do
Tha'll go back.

The poem concludes touchingly:

But tho' we've childer two or three,
We'll mak' a bit o' reawm for thee,
Bless thee, lad!
Tha'rt th' prattiest brid we have i'th' nest,
So hutch up closer to mi breast;
Aw'm thi dad.

Laycock was one of a number of nineteenth-century writers who chose to write in dialect; others in Lancashire included Sam Bamford, Edwin Waugh and, a generation later, Ammon Wrigley, while John Castillo and John Hartley were perhaps the best-known names from Yorkshire. The schoolmaster William Barnes was also writing at much the same time in Dorset dialect.

There is no reason why English dialect writers should be taken any less seriously than writers in other forms of English, though there is an issue which has to be faced: the power and apparent authority of standard English unfortunately leaves dialect in a potentially marginal position, at risk of being thought suitable just for humour or for mawkish whimsy.

Samuel Laycock doesn't entirely avoid these traps, though his work is strongest when his own passion comes through the writing, as in his poem 'To my Son John Edward on his Birthday'. Laycock, in addressing his son, recounts with emotion but without sentimentality the deaths in childhood of two of his other children and then, the bitterest blow of all, the early death of his wife:

> Aw've never held mi yead up reet sin' aw'd that heavy blow;
> An' what aw've suffered i' mi moind ther's very few 'at know;
> Aw connot feel reet settled neaw, whatever aw may do,
> But allus live i' fear an' dread lest aw should lose thee too.

But, having shared his grief with his son, the writer concludes on a homely note:

> Neaw, then, look sharp, be off to th' schoo', aw've towd thi o
>   aw want:
> Tha'll foind thi bag an' slate i'th' nook, an' here's thi top an
>   bant;
> Be sure tha comes straight whoam at noon, we're havin' pie
>   to-day;
> We allus get thee summat noice for th' twenty-nineth o' May.

Laycock also can adopt a lighter touch, as in the poem 'Joe an' Alice', subtitled 'A Yawshur Tale'. It could have been based on Samuel's early years living on the edge of the moors at Marsden. Joe and Alice obviously live in the Pennines, miles from the nearest town and certainly far from the nearest registry office.

When a baby daughter arrives, there seems little need to go through the formalities, or indeed even to give the child a name. Until, that is, officialdom comes to call:

Neaw this couple lived reet up at th' top ov a moor;
It wur seldom a stranger e'er darkened the'r door;
But one day an owd fellow co'd Solomon Crook
Went marchin' i'th' heawse wi' a register book.
He said, 'I've been told by a man I've just met
That you've got a young child, have you christened it yet?'

Joe is busy handloom weaving, but Alice is happy to cooperate and asks Solomon Crook for help in choosing the right name:

'Well, Misses,' he said, 'I will read a few names;
There's Albert, John, Edward, Charles, William, and James;
Augustus, Emanuel, Christopher, Duke,
Cornelius, Jonathan, Isaac, and Luke.'
'Stop, Maister, there's Awsuk; that seands varry nawce;
Aw've seen that i'th' Bawble, aw think once or twawce.
Heigh, Joe! Dusta yer? Stop that weighvin' a bit;
Ther's Awsuk, here, dusta think Awsuk ull fit?'

Joe agrees with his wife: Isaac, or Awsuk, it is. It is only rather later, when Solomon Crook has descended from the moors leaving Joe and Alice alone that they begin to have second thoughts. Alice is the first to raise her concerns:

'What thinks ta, is Awsuk t' reight name for yaar chawld?
It seands varry mich lawk a lad's name to me,
An this babby o' years is a lass, dusta see?'

But it's too late. Joe admits the name might be a little unusual for a girl, but 'ne'er mawnd, it'll do . . .'

WALK 11

STANDEDGE AND PULE HILL

DIFFICULTY 🥾 🥾 **DISTANCE** 5½ miles (9 km)

MARSDEN · TUNNEL END · PULE HILL · REDBROOK RESERVOIR · WARCOCK HILL · MARSDEN

MAPS OS Explorer OL21, South Pennines; OS Explorer OL1, The Peak District – Dark Peak area

STARTING POINT Marsden

PARKING In the British Waterways visitors' car park, beside Marsden station (GR 047119)

PUBLIC TRANSPORT Trains run to Marsden from Manchester, Leeds, Wakefield and Huddersfield. Buses run to Marsden from Huddersfield and Oldham.

A walk above the Standedge tunnels, including the viewpoint of Pule Hill. Relatively easy walking, mostly on footpaths.

■ The National Trust, which owns over 5600 acres of Marsden Moor, has created an interesting exhibition about the history and natural history of the area in its estate office building, in the visitors' car park at Marsden.

▶ Walk along the canal towpath to Marsden Tunnel End. Just before the canal disappears into Standedge tunnel, turn right, beside the Standedge visitor centre ❶.

■ The longest and deepest canal tunnel in Britain, Standedge remains an astonishing engineering, and human, achievement (see pages 114–17). Short in-and-out-again boat trips to the tunnel can be booked in the visitor centre.

▶ Turn right beside the Standedge visitor centre. At the top of the approach road, opposite the Tunnel End pub, turn back left on to a minor road.
Continue, crossing over the channel taking water from the canal feeder reservoir just to the west. At the main Marsden–Saddleworth road, turn right and then almost immediately left to find the footpath heading up to Intake Head Farm.

■ As mentioned on page 118, Intake Head Farm was the childhood home of dialect poet Samuel Laycock.

▶ The path quickly doubles back round a bend. Just after the bend, and before reaching Intake Head Farm, turn right through a gate to take a path straight up the side of the hill. Continue to the hilltop, where one of the ventilation shafts to the tunnels below can be found ❷.

■ Directly below are the four Standedge tunnels, including the original canal tunnel completed in 1811 and the three later railway tunnels, only one of which is still in use. The canal tunnel was originally intended to have thirty-one shafts, although not all of these were eventually constructed.

▶ From here carry on south-westwards, roughly following the route of the tunnels deep in the hill below, until the top of Pule Hill is reached ❸.

■ Pule is a distinctive and prominent hill at just over 1400 ft (437 m). Pule Hill has twice been subject to archaeological excavation, once in 1896 when human bones and two food vessels were found, and again in 1899, when further artefacts were discovered. The vessels are now preserved in the

Tolson museum, Huddersfield. The finds are considered to date back to the Bronze Age.

To the east of Pule Hill is another prehistoric site, this dating back even earlier, to the Stone Age. A set of a hundred tools from the early mesolithic period was discovered here.

▶ Drop down from Pule Hill to the Carriage House Inn below, and cross over the A62.

■ The engineers of the turnpike road between Marsden and Saddleworth tried a number of different routes over Standedge, of which the route followed today by the A62 was to be the last. The initial turnpike dated back to 1759 and from Marsden was routed around the south side of Pule Hill. Thereafter it ran to the north of the later A62 line, crossing Thieves Clough at Thieves Clough Bridge. As several guidebooks mention, much of the engineering work for this road was undertaken by John Metcalf, 'Blind Jack of

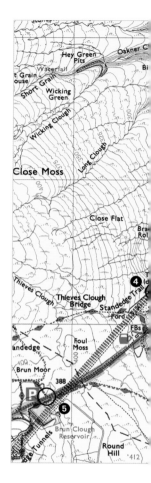

Knaresborough'. His technique for crossing the wet boglands was to clear the ground of vegetation,

© Crown Copyright 100043293 2004

lay down several layers of bundles of heather, press these down firmly and then cover the top with gravel and stone. The road could therefore be said to be carried on a 'raft' above the bogs.

The second turnpike, built in the 1790s, also went to the south of Pule Hill, but then continued further south, running round the south side of Warcock Hill, before turning sharply northwards near the foot of Standedge.

It was the third turnpike, the result of an Act of Parliament in 1820, which created the route still followed by the A62. This new road, opened in 1839, was more highly engineered and suitable for faster wheeled vehicles. By the 1830s, this was important: the road had become a key trans-Pennine route, with regular horse-drawn coach services between Manchester and Leeds running several times a day. The third turnpike ran to the north of Pule Hill; above Diggle, on the other hand, it chose a more southerly route than the previous turnpikes.

▶ Follow the grassy track leading from the A62 to the prominent Red Brook engine house just to the west of the main road ❹.

■ The Red Brook engine house was built between 1803 and 1804, during the construction of the Standedge canal tunnel. It enclosed two shafts and the steam-powered pumps needed for them. The second of the two shafts was deliberately constructed a little to the side of the line of the canal; water was then sprayed down it to help the overall ventilation of the workings. The engine house, which had become derelict, was repaired and repointed in 1993 by the restoration team of the Huddersfield Canal Society.

Spoil removed from the canal and railway tunnels can be seen piled up near Red Brook.

▶ Pass the engine house, and scramble up the spoil heap beyond to find the path which runs on to Thieves Clough Bridge. (This is the route of the first turnpike road.) Take the footpath which heads off slightly to the right, almost due west, on to the open moor and away from the tunnel workings and the A62. After some hundreds of yards (metres), take the left of two alternatives, to join in due course with the Pennine Way, which at this point comes in from the north. Very shortly, you will arrive back at the A62 ❺. Cross the road, and follow the Pennine Way for about ½ mile (0.8 km), until you are south of the Redbrook reservoir.

■ Redbrook was one of a string of reservoirs built to ensure that the Huddersfield Narrow Canal had adequate supplies of water for its top section, which included the tunnel itself. Another canal reservoir, Black Moss, suffered the collapse of its embankment in 1810, which resulted in the Colne valley 'Black Flood' and the loss of six lives.

▶ Just to the south of the Redbrook reservoir, the Pennine Way turns to head south-eastwards. At this point ❻, find the less well-defined path which continues half-left (north-eastwards), around the further edge of the reservoir. Continue round Warcock Hill to meet the minor road south of Pule Hill ❼. Cross this and take the farm track contouring around the hill towards Hades Hill.

■ This next stretch of walking offers fine views down to the old mill town of Marsden. Marsden is particularly associated with the Luddite movement of 1812, when local croppers broke up machinery which was threatening to put them out of work. Croppers were highly skilled (and, for the weaving industry, relatively well paid). Their job was to manhandle the very heavy cropping shears, which were 4 ft (1.2 m) long and used to give a smooth finish to woven cloth.

Leonardo da Vinci had been the first, in his notebooks, to sketch out how a cropping machine might be constructed to replace hand-shears. By the end of the eighteenth century, shearing frames not dissimilar to his design had begun to be manufactured in different parts of Europe, including – in Marsden – by the engineers Enoch and James Taylor.

Faced with the automation of their work, the croppers fought back, breaking into the mills to destroy the shearing frames. In the process they used heavy hammers named after their maker – who was the same Enoch Taylor. As was said at the time 'Enoch makes them, and Enoch breaks them'.

The Luddite protests came to a head in April 1812, when a Marsden mill owner William Horsfall was shot dead. A number of alleged ringleaders were later hanged in York.

▶ Before Hades Farm is reached, drop down the hillside ❽ passing New Hey Farm, and make your way back by field footpaths to the centre of Marsden.

Tunnel End, Marsden

The landowner and the town council

Sir Joseph Radcliffe, lord of the manor of Marsden and owner of more than five thousand acres of Marsden Moor, had a serious bone to pick with Marsden Urban District Council. The council was insisting that the bridleway across the moors west of Marsden towards Newhey and Rochdale should be available for the public to use. They had even had the temerity to erect 'PH Road' markers to identify the track as an old packhorse route and to help travellers find the way.

But the track went straight across Sir Joseph's shooting estate, and this was the time when driven grouse shooting was beginning to be an increasingly popular pastime for the upper classes. As far as he was concerned, this was his private land, on which the public had no right to be. 'No Trespassing' boards were erected, and his gamekeepers were told to turn back anyone trying to use the route. Persistent offenders were threatened with prosecution.

It was the local council itself which eventually found itself in court. In 1908, the future of the public use of the moorland track (traditionally known as Rapes Highway – Rapes or 'The Reeaps' being the name of the high ground just to the north of what is now the A640) was put in the hands of Mr Justice Channell at the Leeds Winter Assizes. Sir Joseph Radcliffe was the plaintiff; Marsden's town council, the defendants.

The council had to prove that the route had historically been available for all to use – a time-consuming and expensive task. Before the turnpikes, Rapes Highway had been a key packhorse route, used to convey cloth and provisions of all kinds across the Pennine divide. But after the turnpikes, canal and railways came, the usage of the highway dropped. The council had to find elderly witnesses who could testify to the court that they had used the route unhindered in the past.

With some difficulty the witnesses were found, thirty-three in all. Two of them, John Hall of Binn and David Wrigley of Badger Hey, were over ninety and a further five were well over eighty.

Their evidence, the town council thought, should be proof enough, and they were further heartened when three of Sir Joseph Radcliffe's witnesses, including the gamekeeper, were not called upon to give evidence. Even so, the judge's verdict was anxiously awaited.

The witnesses had done their job: the judge found that the route was indeed an ancient highway, available for the public to use. But he went on to add that the town council had been at fault in erecting the 'PH Road' markers and in building new plank bridges to cross the streams – a technical trespass, for which the council was fined forty shillings.

Nevertheless, the verdict was received with great satisfaction. 'It was a matter of sincere rejoicing that the right of way over the Marsden moors had resulted in a verdict in favour of the public,' said the *Huddersfield Examiner*. Another newspaper article put it even more strongly: 'The very stones would have cried out had the people of Marsden been deprived of their right of way over the old Packhorse Road.'

The once controversial 'PH Road' signs remain in place today as a guide for walkers, as anyone undertaking Walk 12 in this book will discover for themselves. And now the whole of Sir Joseph's Marsden Moor estate can be enjoyed by all: in 1955, the estate passed to the National Trust in lieu of death duties.

WALK 12

BUCKSTONES

DIFFICULTY 👢 👢 👢   **DISTANCE** 8½ miles (13.7 km)

MARSDEN   TUNNEL   LOWER   BUCK-   LINSGREAVE   BADGER   RAPES   MARSDEN
           END   GREEN   STONES   HEAD   SLACKS   HIGHWAY
                     OWLERS

MAP OS Explorer OL21, South Pennines

STARTING POINT Marsden

PARKING In the British Waterways visitors' car park, beside Marsden station (GR 047119)

PUBLIC TRANSPORT There are trains to Marsden from Manchester, Leeds, Wakefield and Huddersfield. Buses run to Marsden from Huddersfield and Oldham.

A circuit of the moors west of Marsden. Some rough walking in open country, on wet ground.

▶ As with Walk 11, take the canal towpath to Marsden Tunnel End ❶. Turn up the approach road past the visitors' centre and cross the road by the Tunnel End pub.

Take the footpath at the side of the Tunnel End pub and then turn left, to pick up the track running west to Berry Greave and beyond. In due course the track becomes a footpath.

Below Lower Green Owlers, the path emerges at a tarmac road. Turn right, pass the house and then turn left on the track leading eventually to Hatter Lee ❷.

Leave the track just before the last farmhouse is reached, to find the footpath which runs off across the moor just south of a boundary

© Crown Copyright 100043293 2004

▶ Map continues westwards on pages 134–5

wall. Very shortly, turn off the main footpath over two stiles, to take the right of way shown on the map towards Buckstones.

The fact that this is a right of way may reassure, but the reality is that the next few hundred yards (metres) are rough going, with little sign on the ground of any path. However, aim to follow as closely as possible the route of the path as shown on the map (in other words, don't be tempted to make straight for Buckstones House in the distance ahead). Once through the wet terrain of March Haigh Flat, just as the ground begins to rise, the footpath can be found much more easily. It runs in a roughly westerly direction, contouring along the hillside. Stay on this path, as it gradually climbs up to the main road at Buckstones ❸.

■ The Buckstones area is a popular spot for hang-gliders, who may be visible overhead as you follow the path up from March Haigh Flat. Unfortunately, however, the pub which used to be here to fortify travellers is now a private house.

▶ Cross the A640, and take a faint trod running up the moor to the right of the old pub (a fence runs parallel, a little way to the left). Continue ahead across rough ground, towards Moss Moor Edge, until you meet another fence ❹. Turn left here, and carry on along the fence boundary.

The suggested route now follows this fence for over a mile (approaching 2 km) as it marks out the northern limit of the National Trust's Marsden Moor

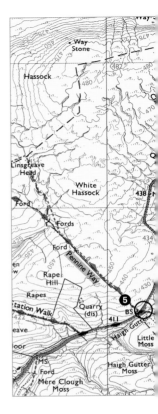

estate. However, some walkers will want to divert briefly from the fence, carrying on a little way down the hill to be able to get the view down to the M62 and across to Rishworth Moor.

The fence runs on, initially in a westerly direction and then turning south. The ground is wet

© Crown Copyright 100043293 2004

and boggy in some places, but
the worst stretches can generally
be by-passed without too much
difficulty.

Eventually the fence passes
the watershed at Linsgreave
Head, and the peaty cloughs
begin to carry the moorland
water south rather than north. In

a very short while, you will be able
to pick up the Pennine Way, just a
few yards (metres) away to the
right. Follow the Pennine Way
down to the A640 **5**.

■ This area, known as Badger
Slacks, is a prehistoric site
dating back to the mesolithic

▶ page 138

135

Eastergate Bridge

(middle Stone Age) period more than five thousand years ago. Francis Buckley, an archaeologist writing in 1924, reported finding 'a litter of burnt wood (ling and birch)' which he believed 'suggests forcibly a rude shelter made of tree branches'.

▶ At the A640 leave the Pennine Way, taking instead the bridleway which heads off eastwards towards Marsden.

■ This bridleway is a very long-established packhorse route across the moors, and is traditionally known as Rapes Highway.

The right to use this route was nearly lost a hundred years ago, at the time when driven grouse shooting was becoming increasingly important on the Pennine moors (see pages 130–31).

▶ Continue down the moor, passing the 'PH Road' markers erected by Marsden Urban District Council in an attempt to keep the route open. In due course, good views across to Pule Hill open up.

Near the end of the moor, the attractive packhorse bridge known locally as Eastergate is reached ❻.

■ Eastergate Bridge took its name not from the religious calendar but from a local publican, Esther Schofield who ran the nearby Pack Horse Inn in the mid-nineteenth century. The bridge is officially known as Close Gate, or Clowse Gate, Bridge.

▶ Cross Eastergate Bridge, and follow the side of the river until Waters Road is reached. Turn right, and follow this past Hey Green restaurant and hotel.

■ It's worth looking out for the old gateway in the wall around the grounds of Hey Green, which has now been filled with a sculpture in iron by Yorkshire-based sculptor Jason Thomson. In recent years, Thomson has also worked as artist in residence at the primary school in the nearby village of Meltham.

▶ Follow Waters Road back to Tunnel End, and to Marsden.

Some further reading

Here is a small selection of books which will tell you more about the area. Please note that not all of these are still in print.

Bernard Barnes, *Passage Through Time: Saddleworth Roads and Trackways*, Saddleworth Historical Society, 1981

Ken Booth, *Roman Saddleworth*, Saddleworth Archaeological Trust, 2001

Ron Collier and Roni Wilkinson, *Dark Peak Aircraft Wrecks 1*, Barnsley Chronicle Newspaper Group, 1979; new editions Wharncliffe Publishing, 1990, and Leo Cooper (Pen and Sword Books), 1995–2000

Ron Collier and Roni Wilkinson, *Dark Peak Aircraft Wrecks 2*, Wharncliffe Publishing, 1982; new edition Leo Cooper (Pen and Sword Books), 1992–2002

A.W. Colligan, *The Weighver's Seaport: the Story of Hollingworth Lake*, G. Kelsall (The Bookshop, Littleborough), 1998

Griff Fellows, *The Waterfalls of England*, Sigma Leisure, 2003

Keith Gibson, *Pennine Dreams: the Story of the Huddersfield Narrow Canal*, Tempus Publishing, 2002

Alec Greenhalgh, *'Hail Smiling Morn': Whit Friday Brass Band Contests 1884–1991*, Oldham Leisure Services, 1992

Paul Hannon, *Southern Pennines*, Hillside, 1999

Huddersfield Ramblers, *More Walks in Kirklees*, Ramblers' Association, n.d.

Lesley Kipling and Nick Hall, *On the Trail of the Luddites*, Pennine Heritage Network, 1982

Meltham and District Civic Society, *Meltham Historical Town Trail*, Dearnside Press, 2000

Meltham and District Civic Society, *Ten Walks around Meltham*, revised 2004

John N. Merrill, *Dark Peak Aircraft Wreck Walks*, Walk and Write, 2002

Oldham Group, Ramblers' Association, *Rambles around Oldham,* Ramblers' Association, n.d.

Keith Parry, *Trans-Pennine Heritage: Hills, People and Transport,* David and Charles, 1981

Robert Reid, *Land of Lost Content: the Luddite Revolt 1812,* William Heinemann, 1986

Gladys Sellers, *Walking in the South Pennines,* Cicerone, 1991

W.P.B Stonehouse (ed. David Chadderton), *The Prehistory of Saddleworth and Adjacent Areas,* Saddleworth Archaeological Trust, 2001

A. Wainwright, *Pennine Way Companion,* Westmorland Gazette, 1968; new edition Frances Lincoln, 2004

The Country Code

An abbreviated version of the Country Code, launched in 2004 and supported by a wide range of countryside organizations including the Ramblers' Association, is given below.

Be safe – plan ahead and follow signs

Even when going out locally, it's best to get the latest information about where and when you can go; for example, your rights to enter some areas of open land may be restricted while work is being carried out, for safety reasons or during breeding seasons. Follow advice and local signs, and be prepared for the unexpected.

Leave gates and property as you find them

Please respect the working life of the countryside, as our actions can affect rural livelihoods, the safety and welfare of animals and people, and the heritage that belongs to all of us.

Protect plants and animals, and take your litter home

We have a responsibility to protect the countryside now and for future generations, so make sure you don't harm animals, birds, plants or trees.

Keep dogs under control

The countryside is a great place to exercise dogs, but it's every owner's duty to make sure their dog is not a danger or nuisance to farm animals, wildlife or other people.

Consider other people

Showing consideration and respect for other people makes the countryside a pleasant environment for everyone, whether they are at home, at work or at leisure.

Index

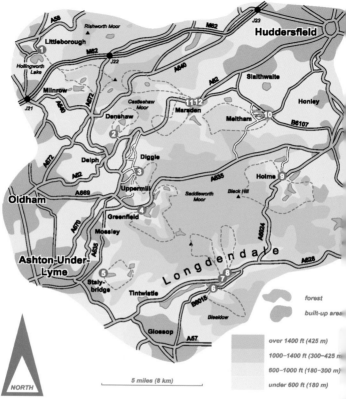

forest

built-up area

over 1400 ft (425 m)

1000–1400 ft (300–425 m)

600–1000 ft (180–300 m)

under 600 ft (180 m)

Not all minor roads are shown

5 miles (8 km)

NORTH